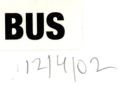

The Official Guide to Body Massage

The Official Guide to
Body Massage

Adele O'Keefe

HABIA
Hairdressing And Beauty Industry Authority

THOMSON
™

Australia · Canada · Mexico · Singapore · Spain · United Kingdom · United States

THOMSON

The Official Guide to Body Massage

Copyright © Adele O'Keefe 2003

The Thomson logo is a trademark used herein under licence.

For more information, contact Thomson, High Holborn House, 50/51 Bedford Row, London, WC1R 4LR or visit us on the World Wide Web at: http://www.thomsonlearning.co.uk

British Library Cataloguing-in-Publication Data
A catalogue record for this book is available from the British Library

ISBN 1-86152-776-4

Typeset by 🅣 Tek-Art, Croydon, Surrey

Printed and bound in Italy by G. Canale & C.

Contents

3 Client consultation and contraindications to treatment 99

4 Preparation for massage 127

5 Pre-heat treatments 139

6 Massage techniques and procedures 147

7 Modifications to massage treatments 165

Baby massage 181

Aromatherapy massage 195

Case studies 233

Tables

Acknowledgements

This book is dedicated to my mum and dad – Olwyn and Eric Shacklady – whose confidence in me has been my inspiration.

I would also like to thank my family – Paul, Bradley and Collette – for their encouragement and support.

I wish to thank the following people for their contributions to the book: Mary Dacey, Fiona Bramwell, Steve Cooper, Angie Walker, Joanna Smithies, Ian Littlewood.

Foreword

When the author of *Indian Head Massage* (also published by Thomson Learning) proposed writing a book on baby massage, I was keen to expand the scope of the book and so was delighted when she agreed to write *The Official Guide to Body Massage*.

Adele O'Keefe takes pride in her industry. She is a qualified therapist with many years of experience in both salons and colleges. Her wealth of experience and enthusiasm for her field is evident in her writing, which reflects her buoyant and vibrant personality.

Alan Goldsbro
Chief Executive Officer
Hairdressing And Beauty Industry Authority

Introduction

Massage has existed in one form or another since early civilisation. This introduction chapter traces the key stages in the development of massage.

Massage is the manipulation of the soft tissues and muscles of the body for therapeutic purposes. Rubbing parts of the body is a natural and instinctive way to relieve pain and discomfort, and it was probably this instinct that led to most primitive forms of massage. Touch is one of the first senses to be developed and is essential to our growth as human beings.

In its various forms, massage can be used to stimulate or relax, and it has been used throughout history for both its physical and psychological benefits. Massage is used to treat conditions ranging from headaches, both stress and posture-related, to abdominal, pelvic, muscle and back pain, either general or as a result of specific injuries like falls, sports and car accidents, and even for stress. From a treatment initially used for its physical or 'medical' benefits, the 'feel good' factor of the therapeutic touch has led to its use as a true holistic treatment, one which treats the whole body and mind.

A brief history of massage

The word massage is generally believed to derive from the Arabic '*mass*' or '*mass h*', which means to press softly. Practised in many cultures for thousands of years as one of the earliest forms of healing, massage is an art that can be said to be as old as mankind itself. It was usually practised by doctors and priests.

Records documenting the use of massage in China have been found dating back as far as 3000 BC. Some of these records, including the ancient book *Cong Fou of Tao-Tse* which describes the use of plants, exercises and massage to maintain good health, can be found at the British Museum in London. It describes a form of massage that involves the use of pressure points and is known as *amma*. It is still used in China today. Early writings of Chinese Taoist priests state that 'Early morning effleurage with the palm of the hand after a nights sleep, when blood is rested and tempers more relaxed, protects against colds, keeps the organs supple and prevents any minor ailments.'

Writings documenting massage have also been found by Hindu priests dating back to about 1800 BC, for example *Ayurveda*. The origin of this form of massage, like that of the Japanese form *Shiatsu*, is believed to have originated in China. Evidence has also been found that the ancient Egyptians used massage for both cosmetic and therapeutic purposes, combining massage with oils.

The history of massage in ancient Greece can be traced as far back as Aesculapas, a priest and physician in the seventeenth century BC who is said to have combined massage and exercise to produce a form of 'gymnastics' to treat disease and promote health. The ancient Greeks believed that massage had potent healing properties, and they used it to treat injuries, enhance the performance of athletes, and induce relaxation and sleep. Women used massage combined with aromatic oils as a beauty treatment. It is well documented that the Greek poet Homer referred to the use of massage in treating war injuries in *The Odyssey*, and it is also known that massage was used by the Greeks in the 776 BC Olympic Games. Massage played an important part in the daily life and system of medicine of ancient Greece.

Herodotus, in the fifth century, documented the benefits of massage, and one of his students, Hippocrates, later credited with being the father of medicine, wrote in his *Corpus Hippocratus* in 380 BC:

> The physician must be experienced in many things but also assuredly in rubbing for things that have the same names have not always had the same effect, for rubbing can bind a joint that is too loose and loosen a joint that is too tight, can make flesh or cause parts to waste, hard rubbing binds, soft rubbing loosens, much rubbing causes part to waste, moderate rubbing makes them grow.

As with many medical techniques, the Romans learnt the therapeutic benefits of massage from the Greeks. Galen, a physician to several emperors in the first century AD, was an advocate of massage in the treatment of certain diseases and injuries. He wrote a series of books detailing the benefits of touch, in which he described a variety of strokes, 'I direct that the strokes and circuits of the hands should be made of many sorts, in order that as far as possible all muscle fibres should be rubbed in every direction.'

Pliny, a Roman naturalist, was regularly rubbed to relieve his asthmatic condition, and Julius Caesar was pinched all over every day to relieve neuralgia and headaches. Later massage became an art which was carried out by their slaves. It is thought it was applied as a substitute for exercise and partly to try to reduce the effects of too much food and drink. It is at this time that we first see massage being used for pleasure rather than simply as a medicinal treatment.

During the Middle Ages there is not much reference to or development in massage. By and large, the scientific use of massage disappeared and little progress was made within the context of medicine. In addition, the religious conservatism of the West meant that 'touching' became taboo, so massage was only practised by small groups. However, with the Renaissance came a renewed interest in the writings of the ancient Greek and Roman physicians, and there was a revival in massage with a basis in anatomical and physiological science.

It was not really until the late eighteenth century that massage was reintroduced into the mainstream of European life by Pehr Henrik Ling, a Swedish physiologist. He is alleged to have cured himself of rheumatism using techniques he learnt while travelling around China. When he returned to Sweden, he formalised a system of massage and exercise based on these techniques together with Greek, Egyptian and Roman techniques along with some of his own. He is often credited with being the father of modern massage as he created today's well known and internationally used Swedish massage, which is far more suited to Western tastes.

All the massage strokes in Ling's system relate to the body's circulatory and lymphatic systems. Swedish massage helps to relieve tension, alleviate fatigue and enable deep relaxation. It encourages the body's organs and systems to function more efficiently and helps speed the healing process for any damaged tissue. Ling believed in combining massage with a lot of exercise and physical activity. Today Swedish massage is far more refined and more relaxing for both the client and the masseur or masseuse. Although the techniques have changed, the original movements of effleurage, petrissage, friction and tapotement have remained the same.

At about the same time as Ling, John Grosvenor was using massage to ease stiff joints. It was probably the Dutch physician, Dr Johann Metzger, who estabished massage as part of medical practice, as he used it successfully for rehabilitation and made his techniques consistent with the anatomical and physiological knowledge of the time.

A college in Stockholm offered massage as part of the curriculum for the first time in 1813. It later became popular in other institutes and spas all over the country. A Swedish institute was opened in London in 1838, and in 1899 Sir William Bennett opened a Massage Department in St Georges Hospital, London, unequivocally establishing massage as an accepted form of treatment in the medical profession.

Within complementary therapies, massage has become increasingly popular and represents one of the fastest growing therapies in the UK. After training and qualifying in body massage, many therapists tend to expand their interests to more specialised areas of massage such as baby massage, sports massage, mechanical massage and aromatherapy (massage using essential oils). This book provides information on all these therapies, although further study is required before practising these treatments.

The massage therapist at work

1

Learning objectives

This chapter covers the following:

- working relationships
- health and safety
- The Health and Safety at Work Act 1974
- The Workplace (Health, Safety and Welfare) Regulations 1992
- Accidents
- Working Time Regulations 1998
- Management of Health and Safety at Work Regulations 1999
- Data Protection Act 1984
- The Health and Safety (First Aid) Regulations 1981
- Control of Substances Hazardous to Health (COSHH) Regulations 1999
- Electricity at Work Act 1989
- Local authority bye-laws
- Inspection and registration of premises
- Fire precautions and acts
- The Employer's Liability (Compulsory Insurance) Act 1998
- The Consumer Protection act 1987
- The Manual Handling Operations Regulations 1992
- The Health and Safety (Display Screen Equipment) Regulations 1992

This chapter explores the various issues which will be vital to good practice in your everyday working life practising body massage. It assumes that you will be working in an established salon; however, most of the chapter is also applicable if you are a mobile therapist or if you are setting up your own business. It covers your rights and responsibilities in terms of both employers and clients.

Working relationships

Colleagues

It is essential that you have a good working relationship with all the other members of staff at your place of work both for your own benefit and the benefit of your clients. Everyone should have a job description which is specific to their job role, duties and responsibilities. This helps to ensure that everyone knows what they are doing.

You should be polite and courteous at all times and never talk down to colleagues. Avoid losing your temper and never ridicule colleagues in front of clients. If you have disagreements or personality differences with colleagues, do not show these in front of the client. Settle any differences as soon as possible so it does not affect your work. Should you ever experience any problems which you cannot resolve yourself, you should report the problem or incident to your supervisor who will take the appropriate action. Most companies will have a written procedure for grievances.

Clients

Tip

Remember, good practice concerns not only the way you carry out massage but also the way you relate to clients and colleagues

It is important that clients enjoy their visit to the salon or clinic and that they feel totally relaxed and comfortable. You should always remember that every client is an individual with different needs. You need to know how to approach them in order to make them feel important and relaxed, and this process often begins before you even speak. Non-verbal communication is very important in service professions such as beauty therapy. Even when we are not speaking we are transmitting our feelings by the way we look and act, for example the way we smile at the client or make or avoid eye contact.

The manner in which you speak is also very important.

Do's	Don'ts
● speak clearly	● shout
● use a courteous tone and manner	● use slang
● listen to what your client has to say, as this will help you to identify their needs.	● interrupt the client when they are speaking
	● use jargon or technical terminology
	● talk about controversial

Tip

It is helpful to make notes on the client's record card of topics that are of particular interest to them. You can bring up these topics on their next visit. This will make them feel special.

- guide the conversation to find out the client's needs but avoid interrogating them.

subjects like sex, religion and politics

Remember you need to gain their confidence and build up a good professional relationship. Often when the client gets to know you they will start to share confidences with you. **Never** pass judgement and always maintain their confidence by not discussing what you have been told.

Health and safety

It is very important to be aware of the different areas of legislation. There are a number of health and safety laws which must be followed whether you are working in a salon, leisure centre, clinic, or you are offering home visits. Health and safety legislation is part of criminal law and employees, employers and customers/clients all have certain duties imposed and owed to them under these laws. You are legally obliged to provide a safe and hygienic environment, and it is very important that you follow health and safety guidelines. The laws are designed to protect you and your clients and penalties for contravening these laws can be severe. It is therefore important that you are aware of the relevant publications which highlight your responsibilities and your rights.

The Health and Safety at Work Act 1974

This covers all aspects of health, safety and welfare at work. It identifies the responsibilities of not only the employer but also the employees. Under this act, employers are responsible for the health and safety of anyone who enters their premises. They must provide a safe working environment in terms of equipment, systems of work, training, supervision, storage, welfare and personal protection. The Act states employees must take reasonable precautions to ensure/protect the health and safety of themselves, clients and colleagues.

The Workplace (Health, Safety and Welfare) Regulations 1992

These regulations incorporate the Health and Safety at Work Act 1974 and also other earlier legislation including the Offices, Shops, and Railway Premises Act 1963, as this is being phased out (although there is a requirement to register your business with the local council).

The new Regulations state the minimum standard of health, safety and welfare required in each area of the work place.

Health and Safety at Work Act

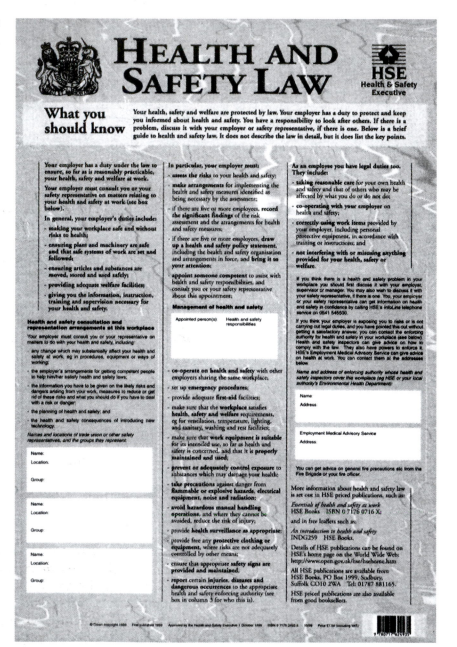

If an employer has more than five employees they must have a health and safety policy for the establishment and this must be available to all the staff. Regular checks must be made in the work place to check that safety is being maintained at all times. It is the employer's responsibility to implement the Act and to ensure that the work place is safe for the employees and clients. Under these regulations, employers must:

- ensure the safe use of equipment and the safe working of systems
- ensure safe storage and use of substances and equipment
- provide necessary training, information and instruction
- provide personal protective equipment which will ensure health and safety
- ensure the place of work is a safe place
- maintain and provide access to the place of work and all its exits.

Failure to comply with these duties may result in criminal liability and a claim for damages. Minor offences may result in fines up to £5000, and for more serious offences up to £20 000 and/or six months imprisonment. Very serious offences may result in fines being unlimited as well as up to two years imprisonment. If a hazard is identified it must be reported to the relevant authority, and then it will have to be rectified by the employer.

The regulations cover issues such as maintenance of the work place and equipment, ventilation, temperature and lighting, access to drinking water and eating facilities, etc.

Maintenance of the workplace

Cleanliness

All areas of the premises must be kept clean and tidy at all times.

Rest rooms

There should be clean toilet facilities for both men and women. In small salons men and women may share the same WC if the toilet is in a separate room and can be secured from the inside. There must be washing facilities near to the WC or urinal, which supply hot and cold water, soap and a hand dryer or paper towels.

Food and drink

If staff eat and drink on the premises then a suitable area must be provided for them in which to eat, drink (a supply of wholesome drinking water must be available) and rest.

Clothing

An area must also be provided for the staff to hang their outdoor clothes.

Salon temperature

The ambient temperature should be 16°C minimum (61°F) within one hour of the employees arriving for work. The working environment must be well ventilated and the lighting must be adequate to ensure that all treatments can be carried out safely with no risk of an accident occurring.

Ventilation

Ventilation must be good, as it provides a healthy environment for the clients and employees. Ventilation allows fresh air to replace stale air, so good ventilation may be achieved by opening doors and windows, but clients may be distracted by the additional noise and also feel a lack of privacy. Artificial ventilation may be more appropriate:

- Free standing fans are usually portable, but only really provide air movement and are therefore not really effective;
- An exhaust system pushes air from inside the clinic to the outside;
- A supply system draws in fresh air from outside and filters it to remove any dust;
- Exhaust and supply systems can be combined with an air conditioning system. Air conditioning units can either warm the air if it is cold or cool the air if it is too hot. If the humidity is not right it can dry or moisten the air to create the correct humidity. Air conditioning also filters out particles of dust.

Humidity

If humidity is not controlled properly and becomes too high, it can lead to problems such as headache, fatigue and irritability.

Lighting

Lighting must be suitable in all work areas, light fittings, windows and skylights must be cleaned on a regular basis, and any broken tubes or bulbs replaced. It is extremely important that there is sufficient lighting for the therapist to work efficiently, but at the same time the clients will not like to have the lights too bright when they are trying to relax. The best solution to this is spotlights, which can be pointed in any direction and dimmed when required.

Glass

Windows, partitions and doors that are glazed must be made of safe materials (toughened or laminated glass should be used) and marked appropriately.

Privacy

Treatment rooms are ideal for privacy, but in many clinics there is not enough space to allow them. In that case, treatment areas should be provided with curtains around them to provide privacy for the client.

Accidents

Accidents often occur as a result of unsafe working conditions or negligent employees. As a matter of good practice, all accidents that do occur in the work place should be recorded, for example in an accident book, regardless of how minor the accident appears at first. Legislation exists with regard to the recording and reporting of more serious accidents.

RIDDOR 95 (Reporting of Injuries, Diseases and Dangerous Occurrences Regulation 1995)

This places duties on employers, self-employed people and those in control of a workplace with regard to reporting injuries, diseases and dangerous occurrences. Unless you are self-employed and the incident relates to you, all deaths, major injuries and dangerous occurrences to employees, self-employed contractors and members of the public on your premises must be reported to the Incident Contact Centre or your local HSE Office/Authority without delay.

If an act of violence occurs in the work place and there is an injury, it must be reported but only if it is connected to work. If any industrial disease such as asthma occurs, it must be reported once you receive a letter from the doctor saying the employee has an occupational disease. All dangerous occurrences such as gas leaks and fires must be reported.

This should then be followed up by submitting an F2508 report form within ten days of the incident. This latter requirement also applies to the self-employed. Any injuries that result in the affected person being unable to perform their usual work duties for over three days should also be reported on the same form within ten days. Any reportable work-related disease must be reported on form F2508A.

An accident report form

ACCIDENT REPORT FORM

Date of accident: _____

Time of accident: _____

Location of accident: _____

Address: _____ Post code: _____

Telephone number: _____

Name of injured person: _____

Address: _____ Post code: _____

Telephone number: _____

Injuries

Part(s) of the body affected: _____

Nature of injuries: _____

How did the accident happen?

Provide as much information and detail as possible. _____

_____

First aid given, record details: _____

Name of first aider: _____

Witnesses

Name/s: _____

Address: _____ Post code: _____

Telephone number: _____

Details recorded in accident record book? _____

Signature of injured person _____

Signature of first aider _____

Signature of witnesses _____

Signature of supervisor _____

Tip

Incident Contact Centre
Caerphilly Business Park
Caerphilly CF83 3GG
Tel: 0845 300 9923
Fax: 0845 300 9924
Email: riddor@natbrit.com
Internet: www.riddor.gov.uk

All reporting should be to the Incident Contact Centre (ICC) at Caerphilly and can be done by telephone (Mon-Fri, 08:30 to 17:00), fax, post or via the Internet. You can also report by telephone and send a completed form to your local HSE office or local authority who will forward the report to the ICC.

In addition to this reporting, an employer, self-employed person or person in charge of a work place must ensure that the following points are documented and kept for three years after the injury, disease or dangerous occurrence:

- personal details of those involved
- date and method of reporting
- date, place and time of the event
- brief description of the nature of the event or the disease.

This can be done by keeping a copy of the report form on file, maintaining a separate written log or recording the details on a computer.

If you have any query about RIDDOR or any other legislation enforced by the HSE, you can ring the HSE's InfoLine. More information about RIDDOR, a copy of F2508 and F2508A and a list of reportable major injuries, reportable dangerous occurrences and reportable diseases is available in the free booklet RIDDOR Explained or the priced publication Guide to the Regulation, both published by the HSE.

Accident prevention

The employer must be aware of any potential hazards and rectify them before health and safety is compromised. Some basic guidelines include:

- All entrances and exits must be kept clear.
- There must be adequate lighting in all areas of the premises.
- All staff should be trained in the use of any equipment.
- All electrical equipment should be well-maintained and correctly wired.
- Power points should never be overloaded.
- Regular checks should be made for any cracked plugs, frayed wires, etc.
- All electrical equipment should be switched off before being cleaned and never touched with wet hands.
- All chemical containers should be clearly marked.

Accidents often involve spillages and breakages and these should be dealt with straight away before further accidents are caused. Broken glass can cause cuts, so the hands should be protected with gloves and broken glass should be made safe before being deposited in the waste bin.

Regardless of the environment in which you are practising massage, whether it is a salon, leisure centre, clinic or you offer home visits by a mobile service, you are working in a service industry and you are legally obliged to provide a hygienic and safe environment. It is therefore essential to follow the health and safety guidelines. If you put your clients at risk or cause them any harm, you will be held responsible and will be liable to fine and prosecution. You must, therefore, be aware of the relevant publications which highlight both your rights and responsibilities.

Working Time Regulations 1998

These regulations came into force in October 1998 and are concerned with the working hours, holidays and rest periods for full- and part-time workers. Employees cannot work more than 48 hours per week averaged over 17 weeks, unless the employee agrees in writing, with an agreed notice period in which the employee can withdraw. If the employee also works elsewhere, their hours must be adjusted accordingly.

All adult employees are entitled to at least one day per week off (under 18-year-olds are entitled to two days per week off).

Minimum rest periods

All employees are entitled to at least 20 minutes rest, if they have worked more than six hours (a young person is entitled to 30 minutes if they have worked more than $4\frac{1}{2}$ hours).

Holiday

After an employee has been employed for 13 calendar weeks they are entitled to at least four weeks paid holiday (bank holidays and paid public holidays can be counted towards these).

Management of Health and Safety at Work Regulations 1999

This regulation requires employers to appoint a responsible person, trained and aware of the procedures involved, to assess risks to the health and safety of employees, clients, visitors or anyone entering the premises, and to take the appropriate action to minimise or eliminate the risks.

If the employer has more than five employees, the named responsible person must document the findings of their assessment, and it is advisable to document the findings in any case. If any risks have been identified, an action plan must be drawn up and all staff made aware of the risks and the procedures that will be enforced in order to control the risks. Health and safety training for all staff must be ongoing.

Data Protection Act 1984

This act requires all businesses that store details of clients on a computer to register with the Data Protection Register and comply with the code of practice. This act does not apply to records that are stored manually, i.e. record cards stored in boxes or in drawers.

The Health and Safety (First Aid) Regulations 1981

Under these regulations, employers must ensure that the appropriate equipment and facilities are provided to deal with first aid and injury. It is the employer's responsibility to assess the first aid needs of a work place which are deemed to depend on a number of factors, including the number of employees, the type of work being carried out and the proximity to emergency medical care.

The regulations state that the place of work must have at least one adequately stocked first aid box, preferably located close to handwashing facilities. The kit should be identified by a white cross on a green background, and as a guide could contain at least the following items:

- basic first aid guidance leaflet
- 20 individually wrapped assorted sterile adhesive dressings

- 4 individually wrapped triangular bandages
- 2 sterile eye pads
- 6 safety pins
- 6 medium sized (approx. 12cm × 12cm) individually wrapped sterile wound dressings (non-medicated)
- 2 large (approx. 18 × 18cm) individually wrapped wound dressings (non-medicated)
- individually wrapped moist cleaning wipes
- disposable gloves.

The contents should be examined regularly and restocked as soon as possible after use. It should not contain any tablets or medication and should only contain items which the first aider has been trained to use.

The Regulations detail the number of first aiders or appointed persons required which is dependent on the risk of the occupation and the number of employees. There must be at least one member of staff to take charge in an emergency and record details of accidents. There should be a list of emergency phone numbers – ambulance, fire services and doctor – displayed in the first aid box. All staff should know the location of the first aid box and the identity of the first aider.

When an accident occurs the appointed person or first aider must:

- assess the situation
- try and identify the problem
- provide the appropriate treatment
- arrange transport to the hospital or doctors (if necessary)

First aiders should record incidents to which they are called. The information included should be the date, time and place of the incident; the name and job of the ill or injured person; details of the injury or illness and any first aid given; what happened immediately after; name and signature of the first aider.

Even if you are not the appointed person or first aider in your place of work, it is in everyone's interest to have a basic knowledge of first aid so assistance can be given when required. Find out about attending a recognised first aid course in your area.

The brief section below simply highlights some of the conditions which you might come across when working as a massage therapist.

Unconsciousness

Unconsciousness is caused by an interruption to normal brain activity. When a person becomes unconscious, there is a danger that they will lose control of the muscles which normally keep the airways open and the cough reflex which keeps the throat clear of saliva and could choke on the contents of their stomach.

If a person becomes unconscious for no apparent reason, you should call for an ambulance straight away. If they regain consciousness within three minutes, it is best to advise them to seek medical advice. If the casualty has had an accident or does not regain consciousness after three minutes, you should also call for an ambulance. You should stay with them until the ambulance arrives, checking and recording the pulse and breathing. If you have the qualifications, you should be prepared to resuscitate. If it is safe, move the person to put them in the recovery position.

If you are not aware of any medical conditions, if possible you should check to see if they have anything which identifies a medical condition. For example, they might be carrying a medical card identifying themselves as diabetic, epileptic, on steroids or with an anti-coagulant condition. Bracelets, necklaces or key rings are sometimes worn or carried by people with specific medical conditions. If you can find any of these, it will help the ambulance personnel to administer the correct treatment more quickly. Any syringes, inhalers or medicines which they are carrying will also provide the paramedic with vital clues as to their condition.

The recovery position is a safe and comfortable position in which to place an unconscious or injured person.

1 Loosen any tight clothing and spectacles.
2 Place the person on their back with legs straight.
3 Tuck the hand that is nearest to you under the thigh with arm straight and palm facing upwards.
4 With the other hand, grasp the thigh furthest away and pull up the knee, keep the foot on the floor.
5 With one hand keep the casualty's hand pressed against the cheek, and pull them towards you using the other hand on the upper leg.
6 Make sure the airways are open by tilting the head back. The head needs to be well back, so adjust the cheek hand, so the head is well supported and turned to the side to prevent choking.
7 The top leg should be bent, at right angles to the body, whilst the other leg only slightly bent. Check that they

Recovery position

are not lying on their lower arm and the palm is facing upwards.

8   Check the breathing and pulse rate every ten minutes.

Artificial ventilation

If the casualty has stopped breathing and the first aider is competent, they should use artificial ventilation. Knowing how to administer resuscitation techniques could save a person's life and prevent brain damage. First Aid courses run by organisations like the British Red Cross or St Johns Ambulance teach these techniques. You should not try to learn these techniques from a book as you may do more harm than good, if you are called upon to use them. The basic technique is outlined below for reference only.

1   Make sure the airways are free.
2   Tilt the head back to open the air passages.
3   Pinch the casualty's nose.
4   Take a deep breath, sealing your lips around the person's mouth and blow until you see the chest rise.
5   Take your mouth away and allow the chest to fall.
6   Continue at a rate of ten breaths per minute and check the pulse every ten breaths.
7   If the heart has stopped (there is no pulse), artificial ventilation needs to be combined with chest compressions.

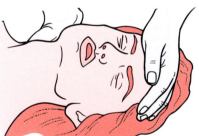
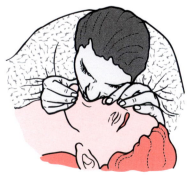
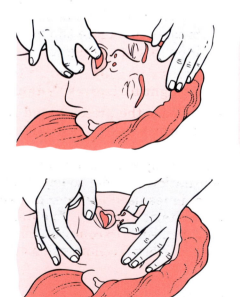

Artificial ventilation

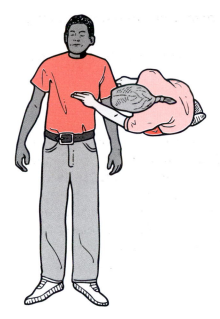

Chest compressions

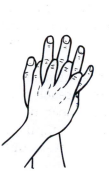

Chest compressions

Remember, these must only be carried out by a qualified first aider. This book should only be used as a reminder of how this technique should be performed in an emergency.

1 Lay the casualty on the floor or a firm surface flat on their back.
2 Place the heel of one hand two finger widths above the point where the casualty's bottom ribs meet the breastbone. Place the heel of the other hand over it and interlock your fingers.
3 Press vertically down on the breastbone with arms straight to depress their chest by 4–5cm.
4 Release the pressure and repeat at a rate of approximately 80 compressions per minute.

Chest compressions need to be combined with artificial ventilation in order to oxygenate the blood. The two techniques used together are known as cardio-pulmonary resuscitation or CPR. To administer CPR the ratio is 2 breaths every 15 compressions, for one first aider or 1 breath every 5 compressions if there are two first aiders.

Pulse rate

In normal adults the heart beat or pulse rate varies from 60–80 beats per minute at rest. This may be slower in very

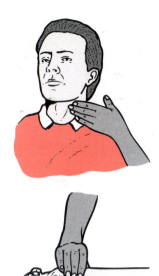

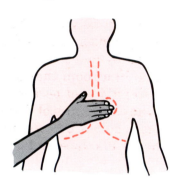

Measuring pulse rate: the neck, the wrist, the chest

fit individuals. In a child the resting pulse/heart rate is between 90–140 beats per minute. The pulse rate may increase with exertion, fear, blood loss, certain illnesses and fever. It may also decrease with certain heart disorders and when someone has fainted.

If you need to measure someone's pulse rate, you should count the number of beats in 30 seconds and then double it to find the beats per minute. The pulse can be taken in various places on the body, but the easiest sites are the neck and wrist. The neck is usually the easiest as the pulse is strongly felt. Using the first and second fingers feel the pulse in the carotid artery, which is just under the angle of the jaw in the hollow between the voice box and adjoining muscle, nearly level with and below the corner of the mouth. To find the pulse in the wrist, you should also use the first and second fingers. The pulse can be felt about 1.5cm in and down from the thumb side of the wrist. The thumb should never be used to take a pulse as it has a pulse itself.

The following are some of the injuries or conditions you may come across when working in massage therapy.

Cramp

Cramp is a painful involuntary muscle contraction, usually caused by poor circulation. It can be brought on by not warming up before an exercise session or through excessive perspiring resulting in loss of body salts. To treat cramp you should stretch and massage the affected muscle as much as possible.

Allergies

Skin allergies occasionally occur during treatment. They can be identified by excessive redness, accompanied in some instances by swelling, itching, a severe burning sensation and vesicles in the area in which the offending product has been used. To treat an allergic reaction you must first of all remove the product which has caused the reaction. This can be done by using tap water. If necessary you should apply a cold pack or a cold compress to the affected area. This will help to reduce swellings or inflammation. If the reaction does not subside, you should refer the client to their doctor. Remember to enter all the details onto the client's record card so that you and your colleagues know not to use the product on the client in future treatment.

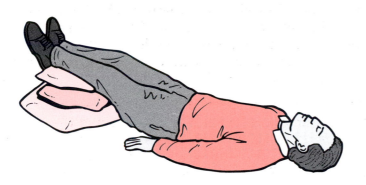 

Dealing with a faint: lie down, sit down

Fainting

Fainting occurs when there is lack of blood flowing to the brain which results in the person losing consciousness for a short period of time. This can be caused by emotional or physical shock or spending a long time in a room that is hot or poorly ventilated. Quite often the affected person will know they are going to faint as they tend to feel dizzy and unsteady. Sometimes they may lose colour or start to sweat excessively, especially from the hands, face and neck.

If the client feels faint either lay them down and raise their feet by placing pillows under their lower legs to stimulate blood flow or sit them down and bend them forwards placing their head between the knees. Make sure that you loosen any tight clothing and instruct them to breathe deeply. Open windows or doors if possible to allow fresh air in. If they have any problems breathing or they faint and do not regain consciousness quickly, put them in the recovery position and call for an ambulance.

Nose bleeds

Nose bleeds may be spontaneous or caused by a blow to the face. To treat a nosebleed, you should sit the person down with their head bent well forwards, loosen any clothing around the neck, ask the casualty to breathe through their mouth and firmly pinch the soft part of their nose (bridge) for about ten minutes. When the bleeding does stop, it is better if the casualty rests quietly for an hour or so and does not blow their nose for about four hours, so that the clot is not disturbed. If the bleeding does not stop after half an hour, the casualty must seek medical advice.

Stings

If the casualty has been stung by a bee, the sting with the poison sac will be in the skin. If you can see this, pull it out with tweezers, grasping the sting below the poison sac and as close to the skin as possible. You should take care to remove the sac with the sting, and on no account attempt to squeeze the sting out as this will spread the poison. You should remove wasp stings in a similar way.

Once the sting has been removed, you should apply a cold compress to the area. You should advise the casualty to seek medical advice if the pain and swelling continue over several days. If the casualty is stung in the mouth, give them ice to suck on to minimise swelling. There is a danger that the swelling may interfere with their breathing, therefore it is advisable to send for an ambulance.

Some people are allergic to bee and wasp stings. Their bodies react in such an extreme way that within minutes they can stop breathing. If you have any doubts, call for an ambulance straight away.

Cuts

If a person cuts themselves it is best to cleanse the area by rinsing under running water. If bleeding occurs, you should either place sterile gauze or a pad of clean cotton wool over the wound, applying pressure for a few minutes and keeping the area elevated. If the bleeding does not stop after a time, medical assistance must be sought. Any cut through the entire skin thickness must be covered with a sterile dressing and medical assistance sought.

Shock

Shock can be caused by many things such as an emotional upset, severe bleeding, a heart attack or some other kind of emergency situation. The face will often become pale and greyish in colour, the hands and face start to sweat but the skin will feel cold and clammy. The person may feel weak and dizzy, and their breathing becomes shallow and rapid. There may be an increase in the pulse rate, followed by a weak pulse rate that appears to come and go.

It is best to reassure the casualty, try to make them comfortable, loosen any tight clothing, lay them down and raise their feet above their head. Try to keep them warm by covering them with a blanket. If they feel sick put them in the recovery position or just turn their head to one side. If you suspect that the shock is caused by electrocution or a heart attack, you should call an ambulance immediately.

Health & Safety

Remember: It is important always to keep your own cuts and sores covered with waterproof plasters to prevent cross-infection from occurring.

Applying pressure to a cut

Burns and Scalds

There are several types of burn, classified by how it is caused. Burns can be caused by:

Table 1.1 *Types of burns and scalds*

Type	Cause	Treatment
electricity	contact with lights, plugs or faulty electrical equipment	area should be cooled with water for ten minutes and a dry dressing applied. Medical attention should be sought as these burns are usually very much deeper than their size indicates.
dry heat	touching a hot object, such as a flame or cigarette	area should be cooled with water for ten minutes and a dry dressing applied
corrosive chemicals	undiluted disinfectants and antiseptics	can produce severe skin burns. It is best to flush the area with large quantities of cold water immediately to dilute the solution
moist heat	scalds can be caused by hot drinks, showers, boiling water	area should be cooled with cold water. Remove anything tight from the area, such as a ring or watch, before swelling starts. If blisters occur these should not be broken as this could cause infection

Health & Safety

Remember: if first aid is to be administered while waiting for an ambulance it must be carried out only by a trained first aider.

Regardless of the cause, all scalds and burns can cause intense pain and are usually accompanied by redness and swelling. Minor scalds and burns can usually be alleviated by the immediate administration of the correct first aid procedures outlined below. Severe burns lead to blisters and the casualty is also in danger of shock, which is directly related to the extent of the injury. Anyone who has suffered severe burns or scalds must be taken to the hospital.

It is important to cool down the injured area by flushing with cold water for about 10 minutes. If this is impossible, for example because the area is too large, it is better to submerge the area, for example in a bath. If neither of these options are available, use a bowl of cold water. Keep submerging the area and constantly splashing it. This will stop the heat in the tissues spreading and will minimise the pain.

If the casualty is wearing any jewellery on the affected area, it is best to remove it before any swelling starts. If a scald occurs over clothing, the clothing should be removed or held away from the body whilst cold water is sought. However, if there is any clothing stuck to a burn, it should not be removed as any blisters that occur must not be broken, as this will leave the area open to infection. The injury should be dressed with a light weight, clean, nonfluffy material. (If nothing else is available, cling film can be used.) This is to keep the wound from getting infected.

Asthma

Making person comfortable during asthma attack

Asthma can affect people of any age and seems to be on the increase. When a person suffers an asthma attack, the breathing tubes go into spasm and narrow so that breathing normally becomes impossible, as they are only able to use the upper lung lobes. Breathing becomes difficult, shallow and wheezy. An attack can be caused by nervous tension, over-exertion, infection, extremes of emotion or an allergy. It is best to keep the casualty sitting up or leaning slightly forward in a comfortable position, and loosen tight clothing. You should reassure the casualty. If this is not their first attack, they will probably have personal medication which they can take. If the attack persists or is severe you should call for an ambulance.

Epilepsy

Epilepsy exhibits itself either as convulsions or loss of consciousness due to abnormal activity in the brain. When a person is having a minor epileptic attack, their eyes become fixed and tend to stare for a few minutes. They become pale and are not aware of what is going on around them. When they come round, they often will not know what has happened. A minor epileptic attack can take the form of a faint. With both types of attack, the person may be a little confused after the attack and unaware of what is going on.

A major attack can be quite frightening for both the victim and any other people present. The casualty may suddenly lose consciousness, remain rigid for a few seconds and then start to experience convulsions. The jaw often becomes clenched, with saliva appearing at the mouth. If the tongue has been bitten, the saliva may be bloodstained. During an attack the casualty may become incontinent due to the loss of muscle control. All of a sudden the person will completely relax and regain consciousness, remembering nothing of the incident.

To treat epilepsy, the first aider must first try and prevent self-injury, by removing anything within the vicinity which the victim could injure themselves on in an attack. Ask onlookers to move away. Do not restrain the casualty but try to protect their head and loosen any clothing around the neck. Keep checking that their airway is clear and they are breathing. As they start to relax place them in the recovery position and stay with them until they have fully recovered, reassuring them if necessary. If they are not recovering send for an ambulance.

Control of Substances Hazardous to Health (COSHH) Regulations 1999

Tip

These regulations do not apply to substances which are only hazardous to health because they are inflammable, although employers and employees must ensure that these are stored correctly.

Many substances that seem quite harmless can prove to be hazardous if incorrectly used or stored. The employer has to carry out a risk assessment to assess which could be a risk to health from exposure and to ensure these are recorded. This must be carried out on a regular basis.

Hazardous substances must be identified by symbols on their packaging, and stored and handled correctly.

Try if possible to replace high risk products with lower risk products.

An assessment should be carried out on all staff members who may be at risk.

Carry out training for all staff members and provide personal protective equipment if required, although this should only be as a last resort.

Substances that are hazardous may enter the body via:

nose – inhalation

mouth – ingestion

skin – contact/absorbed

body – injected or via cuts

eyes – contact.

Each supplier is legally required to make available the guidelines on how their materials should be stored and used.

Hazardous substance symbols

The Provision and Use of Work Equipment Regulations 1992

This states that all equipment must be fit for its purpose, properly maintained, and all staff must be trained in the use of the equipment. This applies to all new and second-hand equipment.

The Personal Protective Equipment at Work Regulations 1992

Usually the requirements from this act are met if you comply with the COSHH regulations. All employers must provide suitable personal protective equipment (PPE) to all employees who may be exposed to any risk while at work.

The Environmental Protection Act 1990

This act states that all waste must be disposed of safely. It is important to exercise care when disposing of surplus/out of date stock and the manufacturer's guidance should be sought. If in any doubt ask the manufacturer to dispose of the stock for you.

Electricity at Work Act 1989

This states that every piece of electrical equipment in the work place must be tested every 12 months by a qualified electrician. An electrical fault can result in an electrical burn, shock or fire, which could obviously have adverse effects on your business.

Local authority bye-laws

These are laws that are made at local level by the local council. If, for example, you want to make major changes to the business or even just change the shop window, you need to apply for permission to the planning department and the public highways department. They will decide if the proposed changes will cause any inconvenience to the local residents, for instance, if parking facilities are adequate or the volume of traffic would increase.

Building regulations

These must be strictly adhered to and are administered from the building control officers working for the local council. This ensures good health and safety for the public.

Fire regulations

The local fire service will provide all the necessary advice on fire fighting equipment and the correct procedures for evacuation. If any structural alterations are made, you must enquire about the fire regulations and carry them out.

Certification of registration

If the business provides treatments such as ear piercing, epilation, tattooing or any form of body piercing, the person who is carrying out these treatments must be registered with the local council.

Licensing

Some local councils require a licence if certain treatments are being carried out such as body massage. These are usually valid for one year and are granted with a set of standards and conditions for a fee. The standards must be met or the licence will be revoked.

Inspection and registration of premises

The local authority's Environmental Health Department enforces the Health and Safety at Work Act. The environmental health officer visits and inspects the premises. Any area of danger is identified by the inspector, and it is then the employer's responsibility to remove the danger within a stated period of time. If the employer fails to comply, this then can lead to prosecution. The inspector has the authority to close the business until he or she is satisfied that all dangers to the public and employees have been removed.

Fire precautions and acts

Fire Precautions Act 1971

A fire certificate is required if there are more than 10 people employed on more than one floor or 20 people employed on one floor at any one time. All premises must be provided with fire fighting equipment, and an escape route in the event of fire. Fire drill notices should be displayed and fire exits clearly marked with appropriate signs.

Fire Precautions (workplace) Regulations 1997 and Fire Precautions (workplace) (amendment) Regulations 1999

This act states that all the staff must be aware of and trained in emergency evacuation and fire procedures for their workplace. A fire risk assessment should always be carried out and the following in place:

- A smoke alarm should be fitted.
- Fire doors should be fitted within the business to help keep the fire from spreading.
- All escape routes must be kept clear of obstruction and there should be emergency lighting.
- Fire fighting equipment must be located in specified areas. This equipment includes fire extinguishers, blankets, buckets, and water hoses, and these should be checked on a regular basis.

Fire fighting and extinguishers

As there are different types of fire fighting equipment it is important that the cause of the fire is identified before using anything. Using the wrong extinguisher could possibly make the fire worse.

There are four causes of fire:

1 Class A fires involve paper, wood, hair, and other solid materials
2 Class B fires involve flammable liquids such as petrol
3 Class C fires involve vaporising gases such as butane and propane
4 Class D fires involve electrics.

Fire extinguishers

A fire caused by solid materials like paper or wood must be extinguished with a water extinguisher. This has a red label and can only be effectively used on Class A fires.

A fire caused by flammable liquids should be extinguished with a foam extinguisher. This is red with a cream/buff label. It should only be used for Class B fires and small Class A fires.

An electrical fire could be extinguished with a dry powder extinguisher. This is red with a blue label. It is also suitable for Class B and Class C fires.

A carbon dioxide extinguisher can be used on all fires but is particularly useful on Class B and electrical fires. It is red with a black label.

Fire blankets can be used on small localised fires and are used to smother the flames. Sand is used on liquids. This will again smother flames and soak up liquids. Water hoses are used on large fires usually caused by paper materials. Buckets of water are used to put out small fires. Always remember to turn off the electricity first.

Public liability insurance

This protects the employers and the employees against any injury or death to a third party while they are on the premises. This is not a legal requirement, but it should be taken out to cover any claims made by the public, as a result of damage or injury to personal property by the employer or employee at work. Every employer must have employer's liability insurance; this provides financial compensation to an employee if they are injured while at work.

The Employer's Liability (Compulsory Insurance) Act 1998

It is the duty of all employers to take out and maintain an insurance policy against liability for all employees within their employment which covers them for bodily injury or disease. The insurance certificate must be displayed in the place of work.

The Consumer Protection Act 1987

This Act safeguards the consumer against unsafe products. The Act covers general safe handling requirements, product liability and prices that are misleading.

The Manual Handling Operations Regulations 1992

Many accidents are as a result of incorrect lifting, carrying, pushing, pulling and handling techniques whether by hand or bodily force. Certain sprains and strains are caused over a period of time, others are a result of a single incident. Employers are required to provide appropriate training for employees after carrying out an assessment of risks.

In some instances it may be just a case of reorganising shelves and storage areas or providing car insurance to enable them to pick up stock and equipment from the wholesaler. Wherever possible it is advisable to avoid manual handling. If this cannot be avoided, you need to consider the following factors:

- load, weight and size of things being moved
- area, whether it is wet or dry and how much space there is
- person's capability in relation to the task being carried out.

The Health and Safety (Display Screen Equipment) Regulations 1992

If you have an employee who is working with display screen equipment, such as a receptionist, you will need to pay for eye tests given by an optician or doctor and special spectacles if required.

It is also the employer's responsibility to provide information and training for display screen equipment users and ensure there are regular breaks or a change of activity.

Knowledge review – the massage therapist at work

1 Name two acts of parliament concerned with health and safety in the work place.

2 What does the abbreviation COSHH stand for?

3 Why is it important to enforce COSHH regulations in the work place?

4 Name six essential items in the work place first aid box.

5 Which fire extinguisher(s) would put out a fire caused by paper or wood?

6 Explain the Data Protection Act 1984.

7 Explain the Reporting of Injuries, Diseases and Dangerous Occurrences Act.

8 Why must regular health and safety checks be carried out in the work place?

9 If a serious accident occurs in the work place who must be informed within ten days of the accident taking place?

10 Why are positive working relationships with your colleagues essential?

11 If you have a grievance, to whom would you report it?

12 What do you understand by employer's liability insurance?

Anatomy, physiology and the effects of massage

2

Learning objectives

This chapter covers the following:

- **basic components of the body**
- **integumentary system**
- **skeletal system**
- **joints**
- **muscular system**
- **circulatory system**
- **lymphatic system**
- **nervous system**
- **digestive system**
- **nutrition**
- **respiratory and olfactory systems**
- **renal system**
- **endocrine system**
- **breasts**
- **psychological benefits**

Massage can have both physical and psychological effects. In order to gain a proper understanding of the physical benefits of massage and perform it safely, it is essential to understand the anatomy and physiology of the human body. This chapter looks in turn at each of the major body systems which can be affected by massage and then explains the effects of massage on each discrete system before moving on to explore the psychological effects of massage. However, you should remember that in the same way that the physical and psychological cannot truly be separated, each system of the body is interconnected and affected by the functioning of other systems.

Basic components of the body

The human body is made up of billions of cells. **Cells** are the smallest structures that show all the features of living things. In multi-cell organisms like the human body, cells combine in groups to do certain jobs effectively. Common groups of cells are known as **tissues**. Different tissues combine to form specialised **organs**, each of which has a particular function, e.g. the stomach. Organs are then organised into **systems**, e.g. the digestive system which combine to form **organisms**.

Cells

Although cells can differ in size, shape, structure and function, they share seven characteristics in common with all living things. These are:

1   growth
2   reproduction
3   sensitivity
4   excretion
5   movement
6   metabolism / nutrition
7   respiration

All cells contain three key components:

● The **nucleus** controls chemical activity and contains the genetic information of the cell. One of the main functions of the nucleus is to control cell reproduction.

Structure of a cell

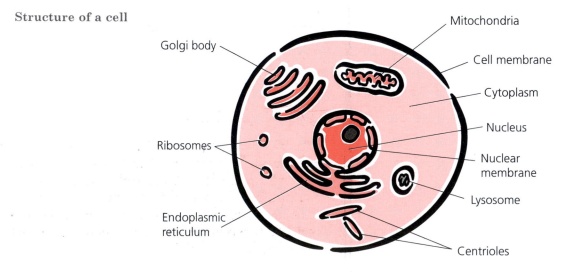

- **Cytoplasm** surrounds the nucleus and fills the cell. It is liquid consisting mostly of water but also contains various organelles as well as salts, dissolved gases and nutrients. The organelles can be involved in energy production, e.g. mitochondria, protein production, e.g. endoplastic reticulum; or have other specialities.

- The **cell membrane** forms the outer surface of the cell surrounding the cytoplasm and controls the passage of soluble substances into and out of the cell.

Tissue

There are four main types of tissue found in animals (including humans) and each carries out a different function. See Table 2.1.

Table 2.1 *Tissues and functions*

Tissue type	Function	Example
nervous	to detect, monitor and respond to internal and external stimuli forming a communication system between different parts of the body	neurones/ nerve cells
connective	to support surround and connect different parts of the body	bones, areolar, cartilage
muscle	to contract and produce movement	skeletal, voluntary, involuntary
epithelial	to form surface linings for protection	epidermis

Nervous tissue

Nervous tissue is made up of nerve fibres and nerve cells or **neurones** which are very sensitive to stimulation. Neurones respond to stimuli and conduct and transmit nerve impulses throughout the body from their origin to their destination. Neurones connect all parts of the body to the central nervous system which consists of the spinal cord and the brain.

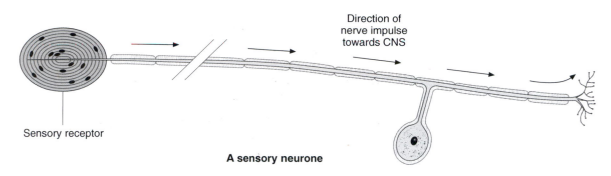

Sensory receptor

A sensory neurone

A sensory neurone

Neurones can be either sensory or motor. Sensory organs include the ears, nose, mouth and eyes, but sensory receptors can also be found in joints, tendons, muscles and the dermis of the skin. When stimulated, impulses pass from the receptor, along the neurone fibre to the central nervous system. This gives us sensations such as touch, taste, sight, smell and hearing. Motor effector neurones conduct impulses away from the central nervous system to the muscles and glands of the body to stimulate them to carry out their work, for example voluntary muscle contractions. Since a nerve is a collection of single neurones (surrounded by a protective sheaf), nerves can contain only sensory neurones, only motor neurones or a combination of the two.

Connective tissue

Connective tissues support and connect various parts of the body. They consist of cells, collagen fibres and networks, elastin and a matrix which can be fluid, solid or gel. There are a number of types of connective tissue including:

- adipose tissue, which stores fat under the skin and around organs
- cartilage, much firmer than the other connective tissues, contains no nerves or blood vessels
- bone
- blood
- fibrous tissue, assists in maintaining the elasticity of skin.

Muscular tissue

There are three types of muscular tissue. See Table 2.2.

Table 2.2 *Muscle tissues*

Type	Function	Location
skeletal	produces body movement and maintains posture	skeletal system
cardiac	under involuntary control and maintains heart beat	only found in the heart
smooth	peristalsis	digestive and circulatory systems, i.e., walls of blood vessels and intestines

Epithelial tissue

The most common example of epithelial tissue can be found in the epidermis (the outer layer of the skin), but tissue of this type can also be found in the linings of the lymph, blood and heart vessels, respiratory and digestive organs. Epithelial tissue can be either **simple**, i.e. composed of a single cell layer or **compound**, i.e. composed of multiple cell layers.

Squamous tissue

There are four basic types of simple epithelial tissue: **squamous**, **cuboidal**, **cilated** and **columnar**. The cells in squamous tissue are like flat stones and fit together closely. They provide a smooth lining for lymph and blood vessels and the heart. Cuboidal tissue is found in some glands and in the tubules in the kidneys. As is suggested by the name, the cells in this tissue are cubed in shape and are found lying in a basement membrane. They are involved in secretion and absorption. Cilated cell tissue is found in the respiratory passages and uterine tubes. Cells in this tissue are columnar, contain hairs (cilia) which force the contents of the tubes to move along in one direction. The final type of simple epithelial tissue is columnar tissue. The cells in this tissue are rectangular in shape and are found in the lining of the gall bladder, organs in the alimentary tract and in the ducts of glands. Some of these cells absorb nutrients during digestion and others secrete mucous.

Cuboidal cells

Cilated cells

Compound or stratified epithelial tissue is less delicate than the simple type. It can also be **squamous**, lining the mouth; **cuboidal** in ducts of sweat glands; **columnar** in the anus, or **transitional** (hollow – found in urinary bladder and prevents organ from rupturing) – lining the bladder. Rather than lining organs as the simple type do, compound epithelial tissue tends to protect underlying structures. The top layers tend to be flat in shape, but in deeper layers the cells are columnar in shape. In compound

Columnar cells

tissues the basal cells are constantly producing new cells by multiplying, which causes them to push the cells above outwards with a flattening effect. These cells are either keratinized, such as the hair, skin and nails, which provide protection and stop the cells underneath from drying out, or non-keratinized such as the conjunctiva of the eyes, the mouth lining and the oesophagus.

Each system of the body is usually built up around one of the body's organs, for example the circulatory or cardiovascular system is built around the heart, the digestive system around the stomach and the integumentary system around the skin. Most of the body's systems can be affected by massage and we will look at each in turn together with the effects massage can have.

The integumentary system

This system is composed of the skin, hair and nails and as far as massage is concerned, the skin is the most important aspect. It is the largest organ of the body and serves as an interface with the environment and as protection for the body.

Structure

The skin consists of three main layers: the epidermis, the dermis, and the subcutaneous layers.

Epidermis

The epidermis, interlocked with the upper layer of the dermis by papillae, is made up of five layers:

Layers of the skin

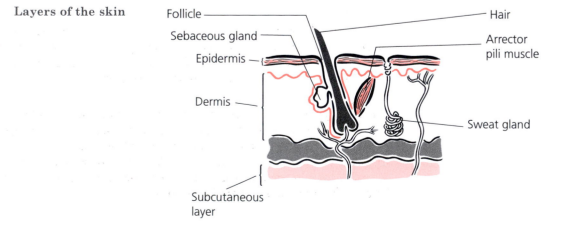

Follicle

Sebaceous gland

Epidermis

Dermis

Subcutaneous layer

Hair

Arrector pili muscle

Sweat gland

- stratum corneum
- stratum lucidum
- stratum granulosm
- stratum spinosm
- stratum germinativum or basal layer.

It is within the layers of the epidermis that the process of **keratinization** takes place. This is the process by which living cells transform to dead horny flat cells with no nucleus. The epidermis contains cells at every stage of this process, from basal cells with well-defined nuclei to superficial flaky debris in which the nuclei and all evidence of cell structure has disappeared. As the cells become keratinized, the epidermis provides a thick, tough outer barrier to protect the body

Skin layer	Functions
stratum corneum	The cells contain an epidermal fatty material which keeps them waterproof and helps keep the skin from cracking and becoming open to infection.
stratum lucidum	This layer derives its name from its clear translucent almost transparent appearance. Only a few cells deep, the stratum lucidum lies between the outer horny layer and the inner granular layer. It is thought that this layer is the barrier that controls the transmission of water through the skin.
stratum granulosm	The thickness of this layer may vary from one to several cells in depth and is at its thickest on the palms of the hands and soles of the feet. The cells are flat and becoming keratinized. These cells reflect light and give the skin a white appearance. Loss of fluid is an essential process in the stages of keratinization, and the cells in this layer are believed to represent the first stage in the transformation of the epidermal cells into the horny keratin material.
stratum spinosum	This prickle cell layer (rounded cells with short projections) is often classed with the stratum germinativum to form the Malpighian layer.
stratum germinativum or basal layer	This is the deepest section of the epidermis and is in contact with the dermis from which it derives its nutrient fluids via the capillary blood vessels.
	It is in this layer that the process of **mitosis** – cell division – takes place as the development of new cells leads to a gradual displacement of the older cells towards the surface. The basal layer is at its most productive between midnight and 4 am and this is one explanation for the term 'beauty sleep'.
	Melanocytes (melanin-forming cells) are found in abundance in this layer with one in every ten cells a pigment-forming melanocyte. Melanin protects the skin against ultraviolet radiation and is responsible for differences in skin colour. Exposure to sunlight increases the production of melanin, as the skin works harder to increase its protection levels. The visible evidence of this is a suntan.

Tip

The epidermis is self-sufficient in reproducing itself.

The thickness of the epidermis can be altered by external stimuli. It will become thicker if it is subject to friction or exposed to sunlight in order to protect the deeper tissues of the body. Radiation, including that from sunlight, damages the epidermis. It causes the upper layers to burn and peel and can affect the dividing basal layers which increases the risk of cancerous growths. If the rays penetrate through the epidermis into the dermis, the connective tissues can be damaged which leads to visible signs of ageing such as wrinkling (due to connective tissue losing elasticity) and thicker, leathery skin.

Layers of the epidermis

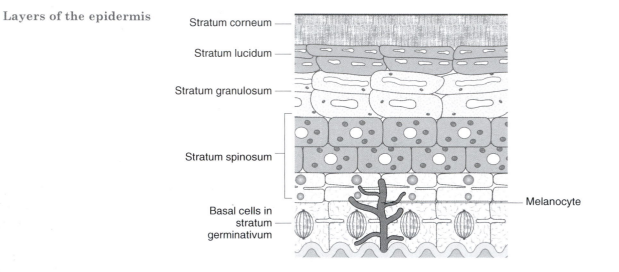

Dermis

The dermis is thicker than the epidermis and lies underneath it. It is a dense fibrous structure which itself consists of two layers: the papillary layer and the reticular layer. The **papillary layer** is the uppermost layer and connects the dermis to the epidermis above. It has an uneven surface made up of fine strands of elastic tissue extending upwards into the epidermis in looped finger-like projections (or **dermal papillae**). These dermal papillae enable oxygen and nutrients to be transported into the basal layer of the epidermis. The **reticular layer** contains fat cells, blood vessels, lymph vessels, sweat glands, hair follicles and nerve endings.

There are three kinds of fibres that intermingle with the cells of the dermis: **collagen fibres**, which make up 78 per cent of the dry weight of the skin; **recticulum fibres**, which form fine branching patterns in the connective tissue helping to link the bundles of collagen fibres; and **elastin**, which is contained within the collagen fibres. Elastin has elastic qualities and helps to give the skin its resilience.

The dermis is thinnest on the eyelids. It is thickest on the palms of the hands and the soles of the feet and tends to be thicker in men than in women.

Other structures of the dermis are now discussed.

Sensory nerve endings

Situated in the dermis, these register any pain, pressure, touch and changes in the temperature. It is the sensory nerve endings that send messages to the central nervous system and the brain to let us know what is happening on the skin's surface.

The dermis contains structures which are called skin appendages, these are

- sweat glands
- hair follicles
- sebaceous glands
- nails

Sweat glands (subodiferous glands)

These glands extend from the epidermis to the dermis and are found all over the body. The function is to regulate the body temperature. There are two types of sweat glands:

1 eccrine glands – these are coiled in the dermis but look straight in appearance to the epidermis. They are found all over the body and appear as tiny ducts which open directly onto the skin's surface, commonly referred to as pores. Their function is to maintain body temperature (36.8°C) by continually secreting small amounts of sweat.

2 apocrine glands – these are attached to a hair follicle and are controlled by hormones. Their activity increases when we become nervous or excited. The fluid that is secreted contains small amounts of protein, urea, fats and sugars and is thicker in consistency than the secretion from the eccrine glands. If good personal hygiene is not adhered to, an unpleasant smell is produced when sweat is broken down by the skin's bacteria.

Hair follicles

These are found all over the body except on the lips, the soles and the palms. The hair follicle is connected to the base of the epidermis by the arrector pili which is a small muscle. When the arrector pili contracts, it causes the hair to stand up in its hair follicle which results in a goose pimple. The hair is composed of cells called germinal matrix formed in the hair bulb (lowest part of the hair). The follicle is supplied by nerves and blood vessels which nourish the cells in the area as they reproduce. The cells move up the follicle from the bulb, and their structure changes to form the hair.

Sebaceous glands

These are found all over the body except for the palms and soles. The sebaceous glands produce the skin's natural oil which is referred to as sebum. Sebum is made up of fatty acids and waxes which have fungicidal and bactericidal properties and also reduce the amount of moisture evaporating from the skin and prevent it from becoming dry.

Nails

Nails protect the nail bed which is the living part of the nail. Nails are composed of dead epidermis cells which are keratinised and therefore hard.

Subcutaneous layer

This layer contains **adipose tissue**. As well as in the skin, adipose tissue can also be found around the organs of the body. It stores fat which is used as a reserve when energy intake from food falls below energy output. It is composed of specialised cells known as **adipocyte cells**. Adipose tissue varies in thickness according to age, sex and general health and tends to be thicker in women than men. The fatty adipose tissue gives smoothness and shape to the body and serves as a protective cushion for the upper skin layers. Massage is thought to aid the reduction of adipose tissues.

Function

It is essential to life that the skin functions both efficiently and effectively. It has six main functions.

1 **Protection**   The skin protects the body from bacterial infection and injury.
2 **Heat regulation**   It compensates for changing temperatures outside the body. Sweat glands make the necessary adjustment to their functions in order to maintain the normal temperature of a healthy body (36.8°).
3 **Secretion and excretion**   The skin acts as both an excretory and secretary organ. Subodiferous glands excrete perspiration, which is a waste product. Sebaceous glands secrete sebum which coats the skin's surface and helps to waterproof it at the same time as slowing down the evaporation of moisture. The skin also creates a barrier which inhibits the growth of harmful bacteria.

4 **Absorption**   The skin only has limited powers of absorption. Some chemicals, cosmetics and drugs can be absorbed in small amounts through its pores.

5 **Respiration**   The skin breathes through its pores in the same way as we breathe though its lungs. Oxygen is taken in and carbon dioxide is discharged.

6 **Sensation**   Heat, cold, pain, pressure and touch receptors are found in the papillary layer of the dermis. Nerves supplying the skin register these basic sensations.

Effects of massage on the skin

When massage is applied, it produces the following effects:

- improvement in skin condition caused by an increase in circulation, which will improve the functions of the sebaceous and sweat glands by opening them if they are blocked;

- sebaceous glands are nourished by fresh blood supply, leading to an increase in sebum production which softens the skin and makes it more supple;

- subodiferous glands are stimulated which results in the production of more sweat and the excretion of waste products;

- desquamation – removal of the top layer of dead cells – takes place which leads to improved skin condition and a more healthy appearance;

- it is claimed that massage can soften the hard fat in the adipose tissue in the dermis and speed up its removal dispensing it into the circulatory system.

Tip

Never massage over an area if there is any sign of skin infection or if it is severely bruised.

The skeletal system

The skeleton is primarily made up bones, the hardest structure in the body. Bones come in many different shapes, depending on their function and are connected to each other at joints by less dense connective tissues, cartilage and ligament. Supported by skeletal muscles, the skeleton makes up the framework of the body.

Structure

The human skeleton consists of 206 bones divided into two main groups: the axial skeleton which is made up of the

The human skeleton

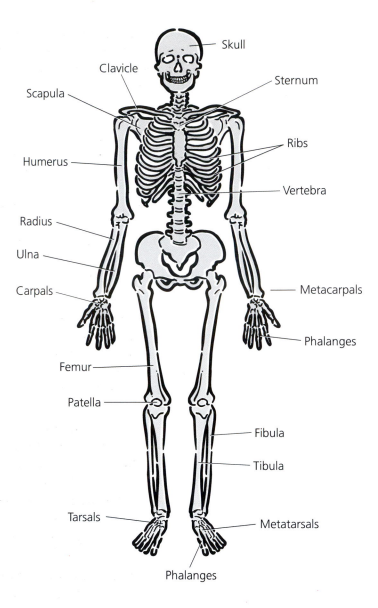

Skull

Clavicle

Sternum

Scapula

Ribs

Humerus

Vertebra

Radius

Ulna

Carpals

Metacarpals

Phalanges

Femur

Patella

Fibula

Tibula

Tarsals

Metatarsals

Phalanges

bones around the centre of the body, i.e. the skull and vertebral column together with the ribs and sternum, and the appendicular skeleton which consists of the bones of the upper and lower limbs together with the pelvic and pectoral girdles.

Axial skeleton

The three main groups of bones that form this part of the skeleton are the bones of the head, the spine and the thorax.

Bones of the head

The skull consists of two parts, namely the **cranium** and the **face**. There are eight bones in the cranium and fourteen in the face. The function of the skull is to protect the brain, and together with the muscles which cover the bones of the face, the skull determines the shape of the face and head.

The cranium

There are eight flat bones forming the cranium which surrounds the brain. These bones are slightly curved and are thin. They are held together by connective tissue. As we grow from childhood, the joints, called **sutures**, become immovable. The eight bones are:

- **frontal bone** forms the front part of the roof of the skull, the forehead and the upper wall of the eye sockets

- **two parietal bones** form the sides and roof of the cranium, the crown

- **two temporal bones** form the sides of the head, the lower region and sides of the cranium around the ears. They provide two attachment points for muscles, the zygomaticus process and the mastoid process

- **occipital bone** forms the back and base of the cranium. It leaves a large hole, the foramen magnum, through which pass the spinal cord, blood vessels and nerves

- **sphenoid bone** forms the anterior part of the cranium base at the back of the eye sockets. It is bat-shaped with wings on either side that form the temples. It joins all the bones of the cranium

- **ethmoid bone**, between the eye sockets, form part of the nasal cavities.

Bones of the cranium

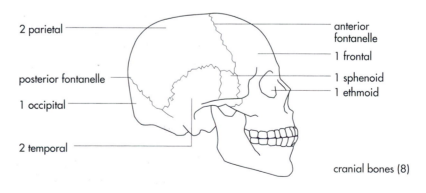

2 parietal — anterior fontanelle

posterior fontanelle — 1 frontal

1 occipital — 1 sphenoid / 1 ethmoid

2 temporal

cranial bones (8)

The face

The facial bones form the facial features and support structures such as the teeth and eyes. The 15 facial bones are:

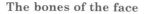
The bones of the face

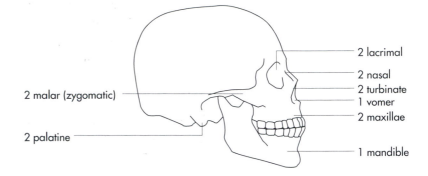

2 lacrimal
2 nasal
2 turbinate
1 vomer
2 maxillae
2 malar (zygomatic)
1 mandible
2 palatine

- **two nasal bones** form the bridge of the nose
- **two maxillae** form the upper jaw, the side walls of the nose and part of the roof of the mouth
- **two malar bones** (zygomatic) form the cheek bones
- **two palatine bones** form the floors and side walls of the nose and the roof of the mouth
- **two lacrimal bones** form the inner walls of the eye socket
- **two turbinate bones** form the outside of the nose
- **vomer bone** forms part of the nasal septum, the dividing bony wall of the nose
- **mandible**, the only movable facial bone, forms the lower jaw. This is the strongest and largest facial bone
- **hyoid bone** supports the tongue (not shown in diagram above). It is a u-shaped bone at the front of the neck.

Vertebral column

The spinal column extends from the skull down to the pelvis. It lies on the posterior side of the skeleton, providing the body with a central flexible axis. It protects the nerve pathway of the spinal cord and provides a surface for muscle attachments.

The spinal column is composed of 33 irregular bones called vertebrae. As some of the vertebrae are fused together, there are only 26 movable bones, they consist of:

- **seven cervical vertebrae** at the top of the spine. The **atlas** vertebra (first vertebra) supports the skull, the **axis** (second vertebra) allows the head to rotate.
- **twelve thoracic vertebrae** lie mid-spine in the thorax region where they articulate with the ribs
- **five lumbar vertebrae** are positioned in the lower region of the back and help support the weight of the body

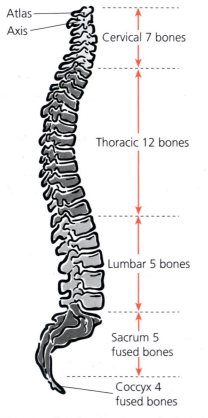

Atlas
Axis
Cervical 7 bones

Thoracic 12 bones

Lumbar 5 bones

Sacrum 5 fused bones

Coccyx 4 fused bones

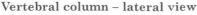
Vertebral column – lateral view

- **five sacral vertebrae**, lie in-between the bones of the pelvis
- **four coccyx vertebrae** are collectively known as the tail bone.

The thorax

The thorax protects internal organs such as the lungs and heart and consists of the **ribs**, **sternum** and the **thoracic vertebrae**.

There are twelve pairs of ribs. The first ten pairs of ribs are attached at the back to a thoracic vertebrae. The first seven pairs attach at the front to the sternum. The next three pairs attach to the ribs above them and are called false ribs. The final two pairs do not attach to anything at the front and are called floating ribs.

The pelvic girdle supports the vertebrae and the weight of the body, and also protects some internal organs such as the uterus. It is composed of two hip bones joined at the back by the **sacrum** and at the front to the **symphysis pubis**.

The sternum is the breastbone, and it provides a surface for muscle attachment, allowing muscle movements and protecting the internal organs.

Appendicular skeleton

Two **clavicles** form the collar bone. These are long slender bones which meet at the base of the neck. The collar bone allows movement of the shoulders, forming a joint with the **scapulae** and the sternum.

Two **scapulae** are the shoulder blades in the upper back. They are triangular and provide attachment for muscles that move the arm. The shoulder girdle, composed of the scapulae and the clavicle, allows movement at the shoulder.

Upper limbs

The **humerus** is the bone in each of the upper arms. The humerus meets the scapulae in a ball-and-socket joint and allows movement in any direction.

The **ulna** and **radius** are the long bones of the forearm. They are tied together by a fibrous ring and allow a rotating movement. The radius is shorter than the ulna bone and is positioned on the thumb side of the forearm. The ulna is positioned on the little finger side. The joint between the two bones produces a movement called pronation. This is when the radius moves obliquely across

Bones of the arm and chest

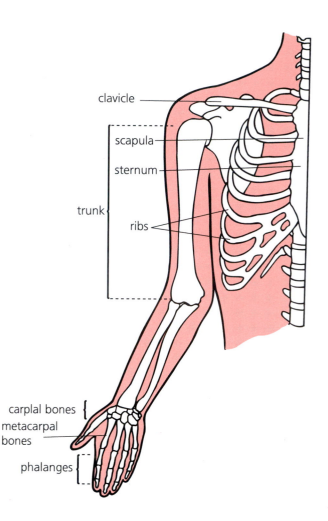

the ulna, resulting in the thumb side of the hand being closest to the body.

The wrist contains eight **carpals**. These are irregular-sized bones which are very close together and held in place by ligaments.

The hand is made up of five **metacarpals** which make up the palm and 14 **phalanges** which make up the fingers – two in each thumb and three in each finger.

Lower limbs

The **femur** is the longest bone in the body and can be found in the upper leg. The head of the femur fits into a socket in the **pelvis**, which forms the hip joint and the distal end articulates with the **patella** (knee cap).

The lower leg is composed of the **tibia,** which is the larger of the two bones carrying body weight and is positioned on the lateral side of the body, and the **fibula**. Both of these bones have joints at the knee and at the ankle.

Bones of the lower leg

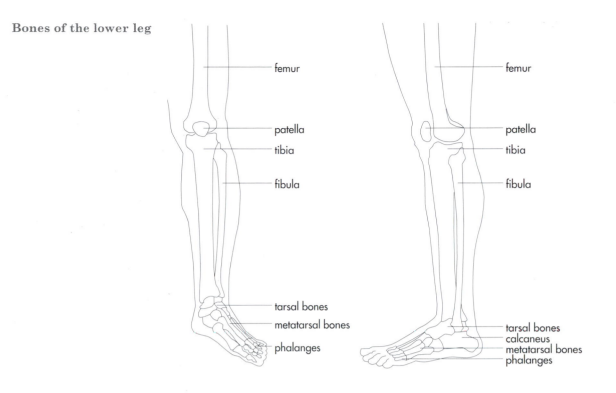

femur
patella
tibia
fibula
tarsal bones
metatarsal bones
phalanges

femur
patella
tibia
fibula
tarsal bones
calcaneus
metatarsal bones
phalanges

The foot is composed of seven **tarsal** bones, five **metatarsal** bones and fourteen **phalanges**. These fit together to form the arches which support the foot and absorb the impact when running, jumping and walking.

Functions of the skeletal system

The skeletal system:

- protects the underlying structures such as the brain, the lungs and the heart
- provides a structure from which many of the internal organs are suspended and kept securely in position
- provides an attachment point for the muscles to allow movement
- supports the softer tissues
- gives shape to the body
- blood cells are made inside the bone known as the bone marrow.

Effects of massage on bones

When massage is applied to bones it does not have any direct effect. What does happen is that because of increased blood circulation the bones are fed fresh oxygen and waste products are absorbed more quickly.

Tip

Never massage over any painful bones if you do not know the reason for the pain. Make sure that any fractures or breaks have healed completely prior to treatment and seek medical advice if the client has any metal pins or discs.

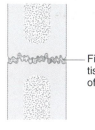

Fibrous connective tissue joins bones of the cranium

A fibrous joint

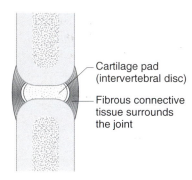
Cartilage pad (intervertebral disc)

Fibrous connective tissue surrounds the joint

A cartilaginous joint

Joints

A joint is where two or more bones meet. There are three main types of joint:

1 Fibrous joints or sutures which do not allow movement between bones. The bone edges are effectively fused together. The joints between the bones in an adult's skull are fibrous joints as is the joint between the maxilla and mandible of the jaw, between the teeth.

2 Cartilaginous joints which allow slight movement between bones by means of **fibrocartilage** pads between the bones which act as shock absorbers by allowing slight movement. The joints between the vertebrae in the spine are cartilaginous joints.

3 Synovial joints which allow free movement between bones because the bones are held loosely together by **ligaments**, a form of connective tissue.

From the point of view of massage, it is synovial joints which are most important because the synovial fluid is stimulated which in turn lubricates and nourishes the joint by helping to increase movement. There are a number of different classifications of synovial joint, depending on the type of movement that they allow. These are hinge, gliding, pivot, condyloid, saddle and ball, and socket. Their basic formation is a sleeve like ligament (or **articulating capsule**) that holds the bones loosely together and surrounds the joint creating a cavity. The capsule is lined with a **synovial membrane** which secretes **synovial fluid**

A synovial joint

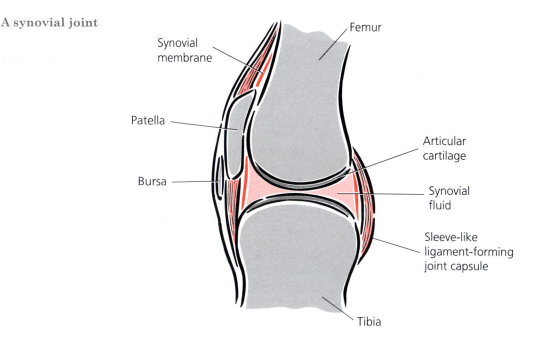

Synovial membrane

Femur

Patella

Bursa

Articular cartilage

Synovial fluid

Sleeve-like ligament-forming joint capsule

Tibia

which lubricates and nourishes the joint. **Articular cartilage** provides a smooth coating that covers the end of each bone, protecting them from wear and tear brought about by friction. Extra strength is produced by the

Table 2.3 *Synovial joints and their functions*

Position	Type	Movement
hand	gliding	**flexion** (angle between two bones at a joint decreases); **extension** (angle between two bones at a joint increases)
foot	gliding	**eversion** (plantar foot surface turns outwards); **inversion** (plantar foot surface turns inwards)
toe	hinge	**extension, flexion**, the joint at the base of the toe allows **abduction** (movement away from the centre of the body) and **adduction** (movement towards the centre of the body)
finger	hinge	**extension** and **flexion**, the joint at the base of the finger allows **abduction** and **adduction**
wrist	**condyloid**: formed between bones of the lower arm which are the radius and the ulna and the wrist bones which are the carpals	**flexion, extension, abduction, adduction**
ankle	**hinge**: formed between the bones of the lower leg tibia and fibula and also the talus of the foot	**dorsiflexion** (produced by the foot pulled up towards the knee); **plantar flexion** (produced when the foot is being pointed)
forearm	**pivot**: formed between the ulna and head of the radius	**supination** (when the palm of the hand turns up); **pronation** (when the hand is turned downwards)
elbow	hinge	**flexion** and **extension** of the arm

Elbow joint

Table 2.3 (Continued)

Position	Type	Movement
knee	**hinge**: formed between the femur and tibia	**extension** and **flexion** of the leg

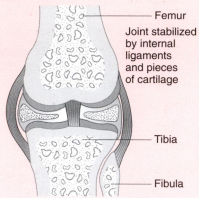

Knee joint

Labels: Femur; Joint stabilized by internal ligaments and pieces of cartilage; Tibia; Fibula

Position	Type	Movement
shoulder	**ball and socket**: the head of the humerus is ball shaped and this fits into the socket on the scapula	**abduction, adduction, extension, flexion** and **rotation**. Also arm circling which involves movement of this joint together with the shoulder

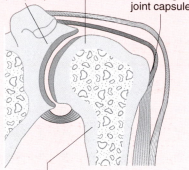

Shoulder joint

Labels: Shallow socket (scapula); Ball (head of humerus); Tendon of biceps muscle runs through the joint capsule; Humerus

Position	Type	Movement
hip	**ball and socket**: the femur head is shaped like a ball and this fits into the pelvis socket	**abduction, adduction, extension, flexion** and **rotation**.

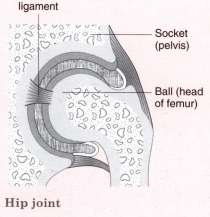

Hip joint

Labels: Intracapsular ligament; Socket (pelvis); Ball (head of femur)

ligaments that run outside the articular capsule or inside the joint itself.

Discs of cartilage are contained in some joints to maintain stability and cushion movement, very much like that found in cartilaginous joints. Some synovial joints also contain a **bursa,** a sac like extension of the synovial membrane, which provides additional cushioning where tendons rub against bones or other tendons to prevent excessive friction and damage.

The main synovial joints in the body are detailed in Table 2.3.

Effects of massage on the joints

Joints are nourished as the blood supply is increased to the area. Massage can also help to loosen any adhesions in a joint's surrounding structures.

The muscular system

Structure

There are two types of muscles: **voluntary** and **involuntary**. Voluntary muscles are used for example in walking, talking or writing; they are muscles that are under our conscious control via the nervous system. Involuntary muscles are muscles we cannot control; they keep the heart beating and allow food to be digested.

There are three types of muscle tissue – **smooth, cardiac** and **skeletal**.

Smooth muscle tissue

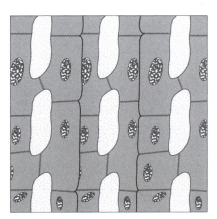

Cardiac muscle tissue

Skeletal muscle tissue

- visceral or smooth is under involuntary control. This type of muscle tissue is involved in automatic functions in the body, for example peristaltic movement in digestion.
- Cardiac is only found in the heart and is under involuntary control
- Skeletal is under voluntary control. This accounts for the majority of the muscular system. Skeletal muscle tissue covers the bones of the body and is attached to them by connective tissue which protects the muscle and gives it its shape. We use it for voluntary movements of the skeleton.

Muscle tissue is composed of 20 per cent protein, 75 per cent water, and 5 per cent mineral salts, fats and glycogen. On average, it makes up about half of a person's total body weight. Muscles are well supplied with blood in order to provide energy, and nerves to deliver messages to and from the brain. Muscles can be either *superficial*, laying just below the skin, or *deep*.

A muscle consists of a number of elastic fibres bound together in bundles. The bundles are usually spindle-shaped and held in a sheath. At the end of the sheath are tendons, strong fibrous bands that attach the muscles to bones.

Voluntary muscles

Structure and movement

Voluntary muscle is made up of cylindrical cells which in turn make up fibres. Each fibre contains several nuclei on its outer membrane or sheath. All of the fibres run longitudinally and form bundles as described above. Voluntary muscle appears stripy. This is because the fibres are made up of two different coloured protein filaments, **myosin**, the thicker of the two filaments, and **actin**. These

Voluntary muscle tissue (detail)

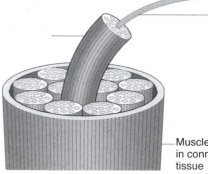

Myofibril

Muscle enclosed in connective tissue

play a significant part in the mechanism or muscle contraction.

Each muscle has an **origin** and an **insertion**. The origin is usually the attachment or most fixed point – **proximal** part. The insertion is usually the most movable point of attachment – **distil** part. When muscles contract, this is called an action.

The attachment of muscles can be by muscle fibrous bands, tendons and muscle fibres, to each other, skin, fascia, bones, ligaments or cartilage.

Muscles work in groups. There will be more than one muscle involved in generating any movement or action. Muscles usually work in pairs. One will be the **agonist** or **protagonist**, whose function is to contract, and the opposing muscle is the **antagonist,** whose function is to relax. Agonists are the prime movers in all muscle action and while the agonists contract, antagonists have the controlling influence. **Synergists** help the protagonists to produce the best possible movement and prevent inefficiency. **Fixators** cut out any unnecessary movements that may hinder the prime movers. They are the stabilisers – they work to hold and fix.

When the muscle is stimulated to contract by the nervous system, a sliding movement occurs within the muscle's contractile fibres. The actin protein filaments move inwards towards the myosin and the two filaments merge. This causes the fibres of the muscle to shorten and thicken and pull on their attachments (bones and joints) to achieve the movements required. When relaxing, the muscle fibres elongate and return to their normal shape.

Properties

Muscle tissue has a number of properties that allow it to function. These properties are:

- the ability to contract and extend
- elasticity, i.e. ability to return to its original shape after contracting or extending
- responsiveness, i.e. contracts in response to nerve impulses.

Voluntary muscles work together with the nervous system and will only contract when stimulated. In order to contract, muscles require energy. This is produced by tissue respiration which is when the glucose, which is delivered by the blood and stored in the muscle in the form of glycogen, combines with oxygen also supplied by the blood. Lactic acid is created as a result of energy production and must be removed from the muscle in order to prevent muscle fatigue. In order to work effectively, therefore, muscles require a good blood supply to deliver oxygen and nutrients and take away lactic acid. If the blood cannot supply enough oxygen, muscles can respire without oxygen for short periods of time. This is called **anaerobic respiration**.

When muscles respire anaerobically, glucose is broken down into lactic acid. As lactic acid builds up in the muscle tissue, it causes fatigue which is not only painful but causes the muscle to stop contracting. Muscle fatigue causes a delay in muscle response and can result in the muscle not working at all. Anaerobic respiration results in an oxygen debt in the muscle tissue which must be repaid. After strenuous exercise where anaerobic respiration occurs, it is essential that the muscles receive a good supply of blood, as oxygen is needed to break down the lactic acid into water and carbon dioxide so that it can be removed from the body. If any traces of lactic acid remain, stiffness will result. Cramps can also occur if the accumulated waste products are not removed quickly.

Muscles work more effectively when warm which is one reason why warming up exercises are advised before participating in any vigorous exercise. They not only help to prepare the muscles, but also improve the blood supply through the muscles. Body massage also helps to improve the blood supply, by relaxing and warming the muscles.

Muscle tone

Technical tip

A certain amount of muscle tone can be maintained superficially by some massage movements

When a muscle is relaxed, a few muscle fibres remain contracted to give the muscle a certain amount of firmness but not enough to produce movement. It is this muscle tension that is referred to as muscle tone, which we often describe as either flabby or firm.

Muscle tone is important in maintaining posture, as it assists the body in standing up and keeps the muscles prepared for action. **Extensors** are muscles that straighten out a limb, whereas **flexors** are muscles that bend a limb. Both the extensors and the flexors need to be partially contracted to keep the body upright and the joints steady.

Firm muscle tone can be achieved by exercising. Flaccid muscle tone is usually a result of a lack of use but can also be caused by damage to the nerve supply. Voluntary muscles require regular exercise. When a muscle is not used, it can become flaccid. In extreme circumstances and after a long period of disuse, a muscle will eventually waste away (**atrophy**).

Posture

When the body is balanced, upright and straight and the muscles are not working too hard to hold it up, this is good posture. Poor posture is when the body is not balanced and the muscles have to work much harder to maintain an upright position. As a result they become very tired and usually will start to ache. Poor posture also affects the internal organs by compressing them, and this affects their function. Digestive problems often result from poor posture, and breathing can also be affected.

Main extensors and flexors used in posture

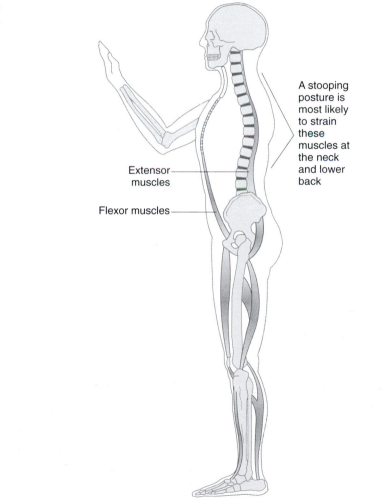

A stooping posture is most likely to strain these muscles at the neck and lower back

Extensor muscles

Flexor muscles

The following tables will detail the main muscles of the body that you will need to know for giving massage treatments.

Muscle groups

Muscles of the head and face

The two groups relevant to massage are the muscles of mastication and the muscles of facial expression. The **muscles of mastication**, which are used in chewing, are attached to the bone and are involved in the movement of the lower jaw or mandible. See Table 2.4.

Table 2.4 *Muscles of mastication*

Muscles	*Position*	*Action*
temporalis	at the side of the head, in front of and above the ear, down to the lower jaw	raises the lower jaw
pterygoid (lateral and medial)	in the lateral part of the cheek, underneath the masseter	moves the jaw from side to side
masseter	in the lateral region of the cheek, between the cheekbone and the angle of the jaw	raises the lower jaw

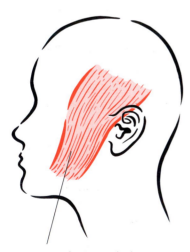

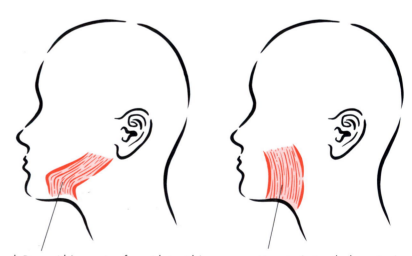

a Temporalis *(raises the lower jaw)*   b Pterygoid *(moves jaw from side to side)*   c Masseter (raises the lower jaw)

Muscles of mastication

The second group are the muscles of facial expression. These may be attached to skin or other muscles rather than bone. See Table 2.5.

Table 2.5 *Muscles of facial expression*

Muscles	Position	Action
frontalis	On the forehead	raises the eyebrows, creases the forehead
occipital	at the back of the head	moves the scalp backwards
corrugator	below the eyebrow	wrinkles between the eyebrows (vertically); frowns
orbicularis oculi	around the eye	closes the eye; winks
nasalis	at the side of the nose	dilates the nostrils; expresses anger
orbicularis oris	surrounds the mouth	closes the mouth; puckers the lips; shapes the lips during speech
mentalis	extends from the lower lip over the centre of the chin	lifts the lower lip; protrudes the lip; wrinkles the chin
triangularis	radiates laterally from the corners of the mouth	draws down the corners of the lip
procerus	on the nasal bone; in the skin between the eyebrows	causes small horizontal creases at the root of the nose
caninus	on the skin at the corner of the mouth	creates an expression of snarling
risorius	radiates laterally from the corners of the mouth	retracts the angle of the mouth; produces a broad (grin) smile
buccinator	at the side of the face	compresses the cheeks; puffs out the cheeks
zygomaticus major and minor	extends from the upper lip	draws the mouth upwards, as when laughing
depressor labii	extends from the lower lip over the chin	pulls down the bottom lip; creates a sulky expression
quadratus labii	radiates from the upper lip	flares the nostrils; raises the lips, forms a furrow. nasolabial giving a sad expression.

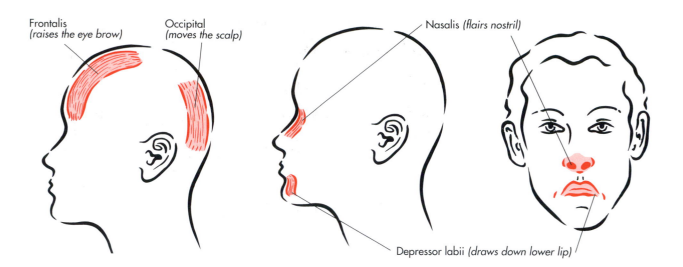

Frontalis
(raises the eye brow)

Occipital
(moves the scalp)

Nasalis (flairs nostril)

Depressor labii (draws down lower lip)

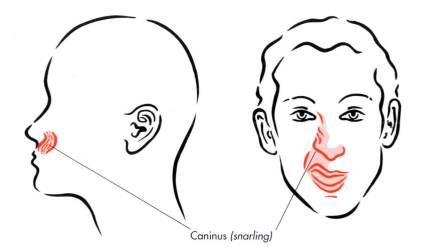

Caninus (snarling)

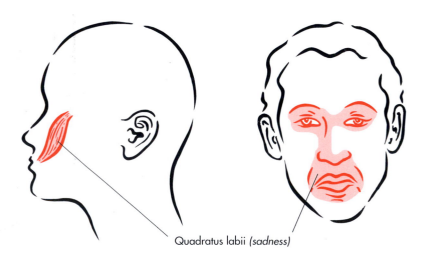

Quadratus labii (sadness)

Muscles of facial expression

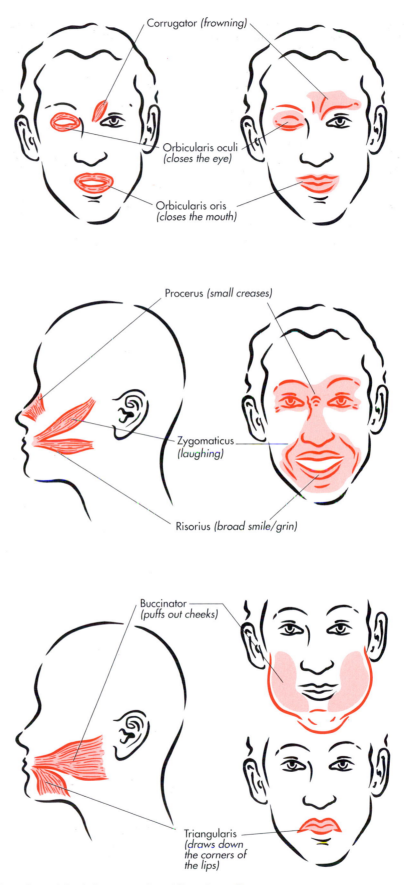

Corrugator *(frowning)*

Orbicularis oculi
(closes the eye)

Orbicularis oris
(closes the mouth)

Procerus *(small creases)*

Zygomaticus
(laughing)

Risorius *(broad smile/grin)*

Buccinator
(puffs out cheeks)

Triangularis
*(draws down
the corners of
the lips)*

Muscles of facial expression (Continued)

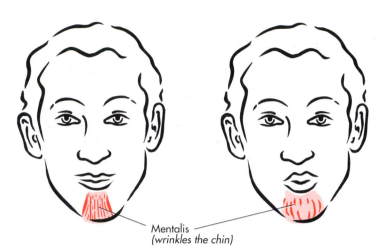

Mentalis
(wrinkles the chin)

Muscles of facial expression (Continued)

Muscles of the neck, chest and shoulders

Table 2.6 *Muscles of the neck, chest and shoulders*

Muscle	Position	Action
sternocleido-mastoid	down the side of the neck, from below the **ear** to the breastbone	turns and flexes the head
platysma	at the side of the neck and chin	helps to draw down lower lip

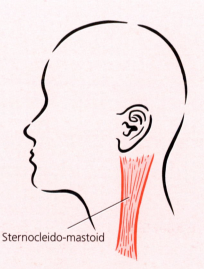

Sternocleido-mastoid

Sternocleido-mastoid

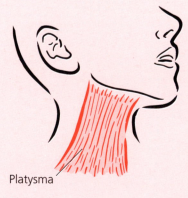

Platysma

Platysma

Table 2.6 (Continued)

Muscle	Position	Action
pectoralis major	beneath the breasts and across the front part of the thorax (upper part)	draws arm forward and rotates it medially
pectoralis minor	below the pectoralis major, its origin is the third, fourth and fifth rib and it inserts into the outer corner of the scapula	draws shoulder downwards and forwards
trapezius	down the back of the neck, onto the shoulders, down onto the mid-spine	lifts and raises the shoulder as in shrugging

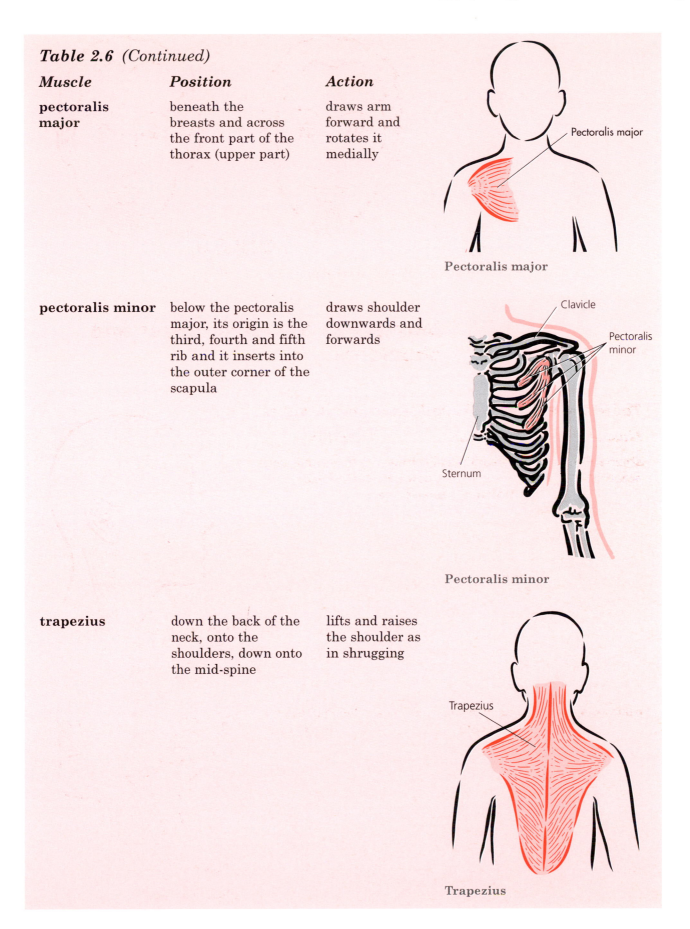

Pectoralis major

Pectoralis major

Clavicle

Pectoralis minor

Sternum

Pectoralis minor

Trapezius

Trapezius

Muscles of the thorax

Table 2.7 *Muscles of the thorax*

Muscle	Position	Action
external intercostals	muscle fibres run downwards and forward and connect the lower border of one rib to the rib below	maintain the shape of the thorax wall. Used in breathing, they draw the ribs upwards and outwards, when breathing in
internal intercostals	lying between the ribs, they run upwards and forwards to the ribs above	draw ribs downwards and inwards when breathing out
serratus anterior	below axilla, along the sides of the rib cage	used when punching and pushing. Rotates scapula upwards and draws scapula forwards
diaphragm	divides the thorax from the abdomen	volume of thorax is increased when muscle contracts

Muscles of the thorax

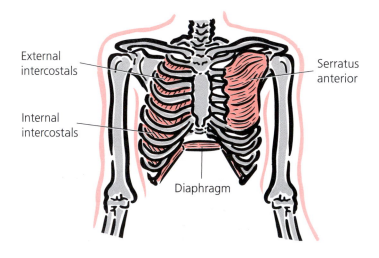

External intercostals

Internal intercostals

Serratus anterior

Diaphragm

Muscles of the back

Table 2.8 *Muscles of the back*

Muscle	*Position*	*Action*
latissimus dorsi	down the back, in the lumbar and lower thoracic region	rotates the arm; draws it away from the body body and rotates it inwards (as when climbing with both arms in a fixed position, it helps to pull the body upwards)
errector spinae	lies on either side of the spine coming from the neck going down to the pelvis. 3 groups overlapping	keeps the body upright; extends the spine
gluteals	situated in the buttocks, they connect the pelvis and femur. Consist of three layers: gluteus maximus, medius and minimus	used in walking, running and to raise the body into an upright position. Also adduct and rotate the femur

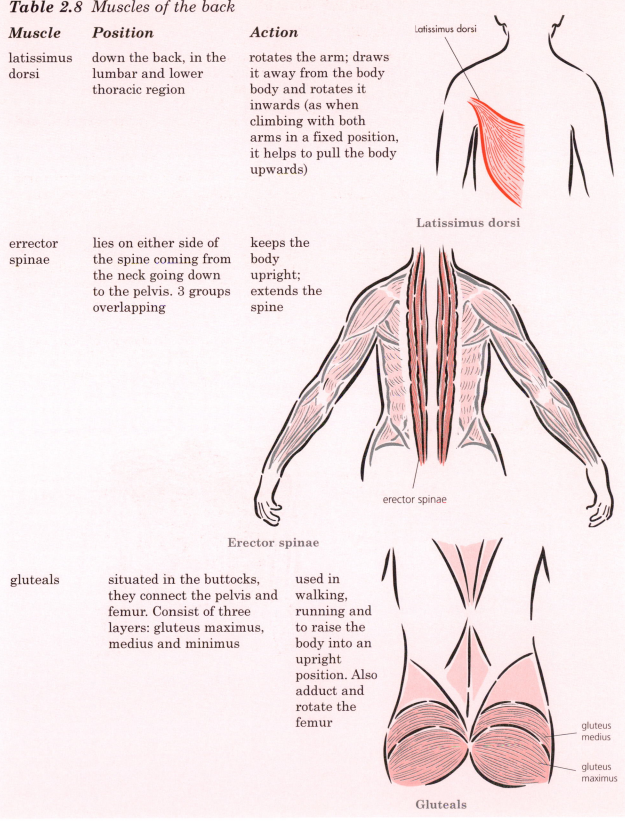

Latissimus dorsi

Latissimus dorsi

erector spinae

Erector spinae

gluteus medius

gluteus maximus

Gluteals

Muscles of the arms and shoulder

Table 2.9 *Muscles of the arms and shoulders*

Muscle	Position	Action
deltoid	lies over the top of the shoulder coming from the clavicle and scapula going to the upper humerus	draws arm backwards and forwards; abducts the arm to a horizontal position
biceps	down the anterior surface of the humerus	turns the palm upwards; flexes the elbow
triceps	along the posterior surface of the humerus	extends elbow
brachialis	under the biceps in front of the humerus from half way down its shaft near the elbow joint to the ulna	flexes the elbow

Deltoid, biceps, triceps, brachialis

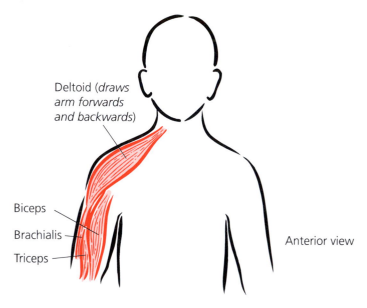

Deltoid (*draws arm forwards and backwards*)

Biceps

Brachialis

Triceps

Anterior view

Muscles of the abdomen

Table 2.10 *Muscles of the abdomen*

Muscle	Position	Action
rectus abdominis	at the front of the abdomen coming from the pelvis to the sternum and the lower ribs	compresses the abdomen, tilts the pelvis up and flexes the spine
obliques (internal and external)	lie to either side of rectus abdominis, run downwards and outwards; external obliques lie on top of the internal obliques, run downwards and forward	compress the abdomen and twist the trunk

Muscles of the abdomen

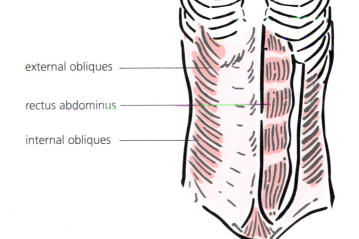

external obliques

rectus abdominus

internal obliques

Muscles of the legs and feet

Table 2.11 Muscles of the legs and feet

Muscle	Position	Action
Quadriceps Rectus femoris Vastus lateralis Vastus medialis Vastus intermedius	situated at the front of the thigh, a group of four muscles running from the pelvis and top of the femur to the tibia through the patella and patellar ligament	extends the knee and helps in hip flex
Hamstrings Biceps femoris Semimembranosus Semitendinosus	three muscles situated at the back of the thigh from the pelvis and top of the femur, down to the bones of the lower leg below the knee	flex the knee and extend the thigh. Used in walking
Adductors Adductor longus Adductor magnus Adductor brevis Gracilis Pectineus	situated in the inner thigh	adduct hip, and flex and rotate femur
Sartorius	cross the front of the thighs from the outer front rim of the pelvis to the tibia at the inner knee	abducts and rotates the femur and flexes the knee and hip. Used when sitting cross-legged
Tensor fascia latae	situated on the lateral side of the thigh	rotates and abducts the thigh inwardly
gastrocnemius	calf of the leg	plantar-flexes the foot and flexes knee
soleus	below the gastrocnemius	plantar-flexes the foot
tibialis anterior	the front of the lower leg	points the foot upwards, dorsiflexion, and allows the soles to face inwards (inversion)

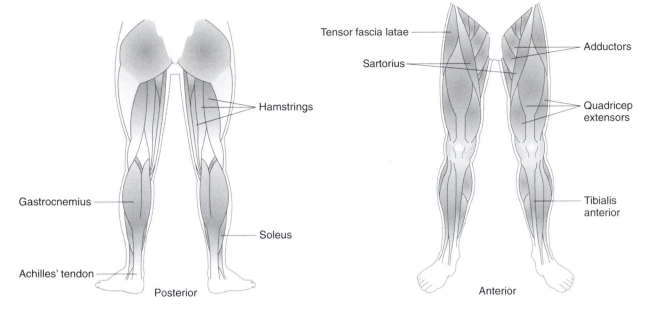

Muscles of the legs

Effects of massage on muscles

Massage has the following effects on muscles:

- Massage increases blood flow which leads to an increase in oxygen and nutrients to the muscle tissues and speeds up removal of waste products. When muscles are working they need a greater supply of oxygen and produce more waste products. Massage will relieve muscular fatigue by removing the lactic acids that build up in the tissues.

- Muscles that are tense and contracted can become relaxed after a massage. Regular massage will help muscles to function to their fullest capacity.

- Muscles work over joints, if the movement of the joints is impaired by adhesions, for example in the shoulder joint, then the full range of movement will be prevented. Massaging this area can help loosen and release these adhesions, gaining more mobility in the joints, more movement in the muscles and therefore increasing the range of movement.

The circulatory system

The circulatory system, also known as the cardiovascular system, consists of the heart, blood vessels and blood and is also closely related to the lymphatic system and its parts. It provides the main transport system in the body, as blood carries oxygen and required nutrients to various parts of the body and removes waste products such as carbon dioxide.

Blood

Blood is a liquid tissue. It consists of a fluid component – **plasma**, and a solid component that includes **cells**. Plasma constitutes 50 to 60 per cent of blood volume.

Red blood cells (**erythrocytes**) are formed in the bone marrow and account for as much as 98 per cent of the total number of blood cells. The primary function of red blood cells is to carry oxygen from the lungs to the rest of the body and carbon dioxide from the body to the lungs. They can do this because they contain haemoglobin which combines readily with both of these gases. White blood cells (**leucocytes**) are produced in the spleen, lymph nodes and the bone marrow. The primary function of these cells is to protect the body from infection and disease. **Platelets** are also found in the blood. They are also formed in the bone marrow and play an important role in allowing blood to clot at a wound site.

Plasma provides the fluid in which the red blood cells, white blood cells and the platelets can be carried around the body. It is derived from food and water taken into the body and about 90 per cent of plasma is water while a further 7 per cent is proteins. Plasma regulates the fluid balance in the body and the pH of blood. The blood also carries fluids and dissolved gases.

Blood protects, regulates and transports materials around the body. Blood transports oxygen from the lungs to the cells of the body, carries carbon dioxide and other waste products from the cells to the lungs, kidneys and sweat glands. It transports nutrients from the digestive system to body cells, carries hormones from the endocrine glands to cells of the body and also transports enzymes around the body. It regulates the pH of the body, helps to regulate body temperature (by **vasoconstriction** and **vasodilation**) and protects the body from disease and infection.

The heart

The heart is the organ at the centre of the circulatory system. It acts as a pump by contracting and forcing the blood through a closed network of blood vessels. It is made

Technical tip

The skin may hold as much as one half of all the blood in the body!

The heart

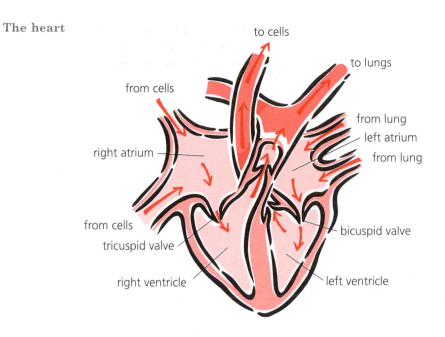

up of cardiac muscle tissue and is positioned above the diaphragm, between the lungs, in the thorax. It is a hollow organ about the size of a fist and it has four chambers: the right and left atria and the right and left ventricles. The right and left sides of the heart are divided by the septum and the atria are connected to the corresponding ventricles by a valve.

During diastole the heart relaxes and it fills with blood from the veins. During systole the heart contracts, and contractions of the atria and the ventricles force blood out of the heart through the arteries.

The heart is made up of three layers:

1   **Pericardium** (outer covering)
    This is a double-layered bag which encloses a cavity filled with pericardial fluid. This reduces friction when the heart beats.

2   **Myocardium** (middle covering)
    This makes up the bulk of the heart and is made of cardiac muscle.

3   **Endocardium** (inner covering)
    This layer covers the heart cavities with blood vessels.

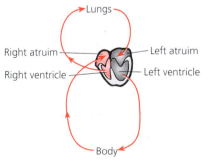

Circulation of blood – overview

Blood vessels

There are three main types of blood vessels – arteries, veins and capillaries. Between them they transport blood around the body and back again.

Artery	Capillary	Vein

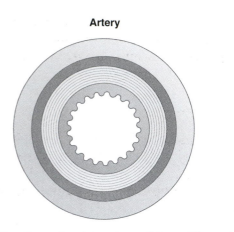 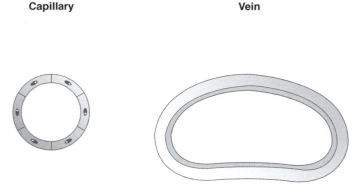

Blood vessles (a) artery, (b) capillary (c) vein

Arteries

Arteries are thick walled blood vessels. With the exception of the **pulmonary artery**, arteries carry oxygenated blood away from the heart, transporting oxygen and nutrients to various parts of the body. When the heart contracts, blood is pushed through the arteries and this can be felt as a **pulse**.

Arteries vary in size from the **aorta** which is the vessel through which oxygenated blood leaves the heart and is about 2 cm in diameter, to microscopic arterioles. These branch into smaller and smaller vessels as they get further away from the heart.

Arteries supply blood to the organs at high pressures, hence their thick, elastic walls, while smaller arterioles control the blood flow through the capillary bed. The smooth muscles in the walls of the arteries and arterioles are richly supplied in nerves which contract to constrict the size of the **lumen** – the cavity through which the blood flows – and therefore increase blood flow.

Blood flow through the muscles is also controlled by this process. During exercise when muscles are contracting, blood flow is increased as increasing supplies of oxygen and glucose are required and increased waste products – mainly carbon dioxide, heat and lactic acid – are produced and need to be carried away.

Capillaries

From the arterioles, blood flows into the capillaries which are thin vessels (single cell layer) and do not contain valves. The main function of capillaries is to take nutrients and amino acids from the blood to the tissues and remove waste products from the tissues. Once exchange of oxygen and nutrients has taken place and the blood has picked up any waste products, the capillaries become larger vessels called venules and then veins.

Vasodilation and vasoconstriction

The skin capillaries help to regulate body temperature. If the body temperature begins to rise, the capillaries in the skin open up, allowing the blood to flow closer to the skin's surface. This is called vasoconstriction. Heat is lost through the skin, and the blood and body are cooled. Conversely, if body temperature begins to drop, the blood can flow deeper releasing less heat into the environment and maintaining body temperature more efficiently. This is called vasodilation. Vasoconstriction and vasodilation are controlled by the autonomic nervous system – nerves that control the arterioles that feed the capillary network for the skin. Impulses from the vaso motor nerves cause the muscles to contract, reducing the diameter of the vessel. When the nerve impulses are inhibited, the muscles relax and the vessels enlarge. In this way the nerve impulses control the flow of blood to the tissues in direct proportion to the tissue's needs.

Vasoconstriction and vasodilation

Blood flow through skin when hot   **and when cold**

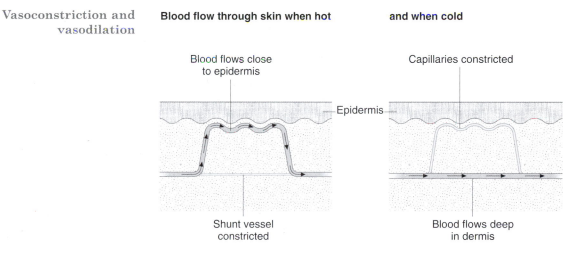

Blood flows close to epidermis

Capillaries constricted

Epidermis

Shunt vessel constricted

Blood flows deep in dermis

Veins

Veins have much thinner walls than arteries and are less elastic. They are also closer to the skin's surface. With the exception of the aorta, veins carry de-oxygenated blood back to the heart along with the waste products of metabolism, which are then passed from the blood to the lungs and exhaled. Venules are the microscopic vessels that continue from the capillaries and merge to form veins. The flow of blood in veins is slower and under less pressure than the

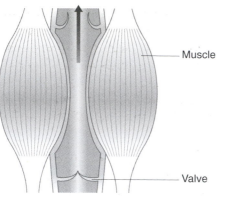

Muscle

Muscles squeeze
the blood in the
veins back towards
the heart

Valve

Varicose veins

A vasicose vein
allows blood to
flow backwards

The walls become
distended so the
valve can not work

flow in arteries. When muscles contract and exert pressure on the veins, the veins tend to collapse. As this happens repeatedly, the blood is forced along towards the heart, valves prevent the blood from flowing backwards.

Varicose veins are the result of valves that are incompetent and allow the blood to flow backward which then stretches and weakens the walls of the veins. The veins on the surface of the leg are the most commonly affected as gravity forces the blood back down the leg.

Blood pressure

Blood pressure is lower in the veins than in the arteries. Blood pressure is recorded by two figures: systolic (when the heart contracts) and diastolic (when the heart relaxes). The blood pressure of an average, healthy male adult should be approximately 120 (systolic pressure) over 80 (diastolic pressure) which is written as

$\frac{120}{80}$ mm/tg.

Blood pressure tends to vary with age, weight and sex and is also affected by exercise, stress and anxiety.

Blood circulation

There are two main types of circulation: pulmonary circulation between the lungs and the heart, and systemic or general circulation between the heart and the rest of the body.

Oxygenated blood leaves the heart from the left ventricle via the aorta, carrying both nutrients and oxygen to all parts of the body via the vast network of arteries. As the blood delivers oxygen and nutrients, it picks up waste products from the liver and transports them along to the kidneys to be eliminated as urine. As well as supplying oxygen and nutrients, the blood also picks up hormones from the pituitary, adrenal and sex glands and delivers them to their destinations – the skin, hair, heart, muscles and brain. Having delivered these vital 'materials', the blood continues to the right atrium via the inferior and superior vena cavae.

The deoxygenated blood, loaded with carbon dioxide, then passes through the tricuspid valve into the right ventricle. It then travels via the pulmonary artery to the lungs where the carbon dioxide from the blood is extracted and exhaled, refuelled with oxygen. The oxygenated blood then leaves the lungs via the pulmonary vein and enters the left atrium where it passes through the bicuspid valve to the left ventricle and embarks on systemic circulation.

Circulation of blood – detail

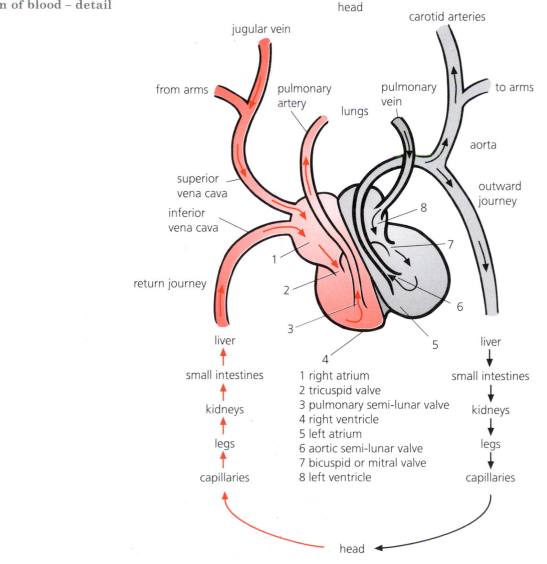

1 right atrium
2 tricuspid valve
3 pulmonary semi-lunar valve
4 right ventricle
5 left atrium
6 aortic semi-lunar valve
7 bicuspid or mitral valve
8 left ventricle

Effects of massage on circulatory system

Massage has the following effects on the circulation:

- Blood supply increases resulting in higher surface temperature of the treated area and an erythema on the skin's surface.

- Cells become healthier and the metabolic rate improves due to faster elimination of waste, toxins and carbon dioxide.

- The tissue is better nourished and improves in condition with faster recovery and repair due to the increase in nutrients.

- It has been suggested that massage can help lower blood pressure caused by stress and anxiety as it has a relaxing effect causing the pulse rate to slow.

Health & Safety

Never massage over varicose veins or areas of deep venous thrombosis.

The lymphatic system

The lymphatic system consists of the lymph fluid, lymph vessels and lymph glands (or nodes.) It is closely related to the blood circulation system but unlike the blood circulation system, it has no muscular pump. The lymph moves through the vessels and around the body when large muscles squeeze the vessels. Lymph travels in one direction only, from body tissue back towards the heart.

The main functions of the lymphatic systems are to:

- remove bacteria and other foreign material
- help prevent infection
- drain away excess fluids which are then eliminated from the body.

Lymph is a clear, colourless watery fluid similar to blood plasma. It contains nutrients, including fatty acids, glucose, amino acids, mineral ions, dissolved oxygen and hormones, all of which are necessary to the health and growth of tissues. Lymph is filtered through the walls of the capillaries. In the spaces between the cells where there are no blood capillaries, lymph provides nourishment. It also removes excess carbon dioxide and nitrogen waste, which cannot be carried by the blood. It also carries a type of white blood cell called **lymphocytes**. A second type of white blood cell, monocytes, is also carried.

Tip

During body massage, the lymph flow is stimulated and also the removal of waste products.

Tip

It is extremely important when massaging to ensure the movements are directing the blood and lymph flow back towards the heart.

The lymphatic system

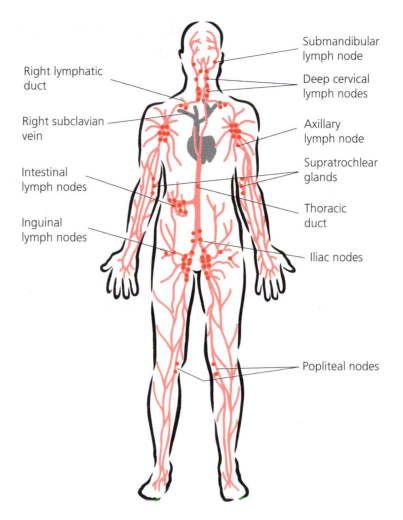

Right lymphatic duct

Right subclavian vein

Intestinal lymph nodes

Inguinal lymph nodes

Submandibular lymph node

Deep cervical lymph nodes

Axillary lymph node

Supratrochlear glands

Thoracic duct

Iliac nodes

Popliteal nodes

Monocytes or **macrophages** line the walls of the lymph nodes and destroy and engulf any debris, bacteria or foreign bodies carried in the lymph. They also manufacture antibodies to fight bacteria, which pass into the blood stream along with the circulating lymph. When we suffer from an infection, the lymph nodes nearest to the infectious site swell, and as the white cells fight the germs, the area becomes tender.

Lymph vessels

Lymph vessels, like veins, have valves along their length to prevent lymph flowing backwards. The vessels run very close to the veins around the body. The vessels join to form larger lymph vessels, and eventually flow into one of two large lymphatic vessels, the **thoracic duct** (or left lymphatic duct) and the **right lymphatic duct**. The right lymphatic duct receives lymph from the right side of the head and upper body; the thoracic duct receives lymph from the left side of the head, the neck, the chest, the abdomen

Lymph

A lymph vessel

and the lower body. These large lymph vessels empty their contents into a vein at the base of the neck, which in turn empties into the **vena cava**. The lymph is mixed into the venous blood as it returns to the heart.

Lymph nodes

Lymph nodes, usually called glands, are tiny oval structures usually between 1mm and 25mm in length, which filter the lymph. They extract poisons and bacteria, defending the body against infection by destroying harmful organisms. **Lymphocytes**, cells found in the lymph glands, produce **antibodies** which fight against the invasion of any micro-organisms.

A lymph node

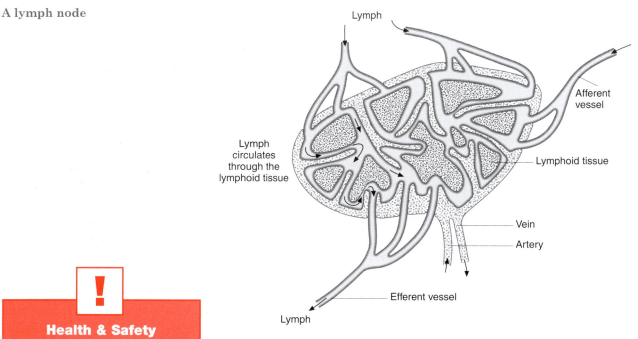

Effects of massage on lymphatic circulation

Massage stimulates and increases lymphatic circulation. This leads to faster removal of waste products like carbon dioxide and lactic acid which helps prevent fatigue.

The nervous system

The nervous system acts as a communication system, carrying messages around the body to control other systems. It enables you to sense any changes inside or outside the body and to respond to them. It works with the endocrine system to maintain homeostasis or a stable condition.

The nervous system includes

- the **brain**, which is protected by the surrounding bones of the cranium,
- the **spinal cord**, which passes through the vertebrae bones of the spinal column,
- and a large number of **nerves** all over the body.

The brain and the spinal cord make up the **central nervous system** (CNS), and 12 pairs of cranial nerves

Table 2.12 *Brain function*

Area of brain	Position	Function
cerebellum	present at the back of the brain, it has two lateral wings shaped like a butterfly	maintains posture and controls motor skills (motor co-ordinating centre)
cerebrum	major part of the brain. Consists of two hemispheres	this is the centre of memory, thought and intelligence. Controls all voluntary muscular movement, receives all sensory information, enabling us to feel, smell, hear, see and taste.
medulla oblongata	this is a continuation of the spinal cord	controls all the autonomic nervous system, such as the heart rate and movement of food through the body. Also controls involuntary reflexes such as swallowing, coughing and sneezing.
hypothalamus	positioned above the pituitary gland, to which it is linked	controls body temperature, hunger and thirst
ventricle	this contains cerebrospinal fluid and is a cavity in the brain	the fluid removes waste, acts as a shock absorber and delivers nutrients

arising from the brain and 31 pairs of spinal nerves arising from the spinal cord make up the **peripheral nervous system**. All sensations from the body are relayed by the peripheral nervous system to the central nervous system, where the appropriate reaction is initiated.

The brain is composed of several parts and each performs specific functions. For example the cerebrum receives sensory information and initiates and controls all muscular movement.

Nerves

A nerve is a collection of nerve fibres that emerge from the central nervous system. Sensory nerves are linked to sensory receptors, while motor nerves end in a gland or muscle. Some nerves contain only sensory nerve fibres which receive information and then relay it to the brain; some nerves contain only motor nerve fibres, which act on information received from the brain, while some nerves contain a combination of the two.

The inside and outside of the membrane of nerve fibres are charged. Messages are passed along the nerve fibres in the form of electrical impulses, which are caused by changes to

> **Tip**
>
> When massage is applied to the body, effects on the nervous system are usually either relaxing or stimulating.

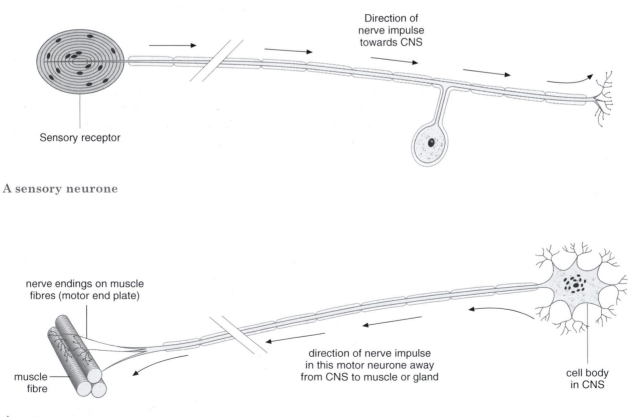

Direction of nerve impulse towards CNS

Sensory receptor

A sensory neurone

nerve endings on muscle fibres (motor end plate)

muscle fibre

direction of nerve impulse in this motor neurone away from CNS to muscle or gland

cell body in CNS

A motor neurone

these charges. When a nerve fibre is resting, i.e. not conducting any message, there are more positive ions present on the outer surface and more negative ions present inside the membrane, and it is said to be polarised. When the neurone is stimulated, a wave of depolarisation passes along the fibre as the charges become temporarily reversed. Potassium and sodium ions present in all the body fluids are positively charged, whereas chloride ions are negatively charged.

Conduction of nerve impulses

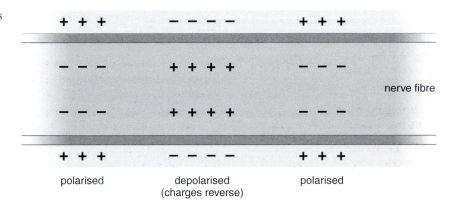

polarised   depolarised   polarised
(charges reverse)

nerve fibre

Relaying messages

Passage from one neurone to another

Neurones (nerve fibres) pass information to and from the central nervous system. Inside the central nervous system, impulses pass from one neurone to another even though they never physically touch. When an impulse reaches the end of the nerve fibre, a chemical called a neurotransmitter is released. This chemical then passes into the gap between one neurone and the next (known as a synapse) before

Passage of an impulse across a synapse

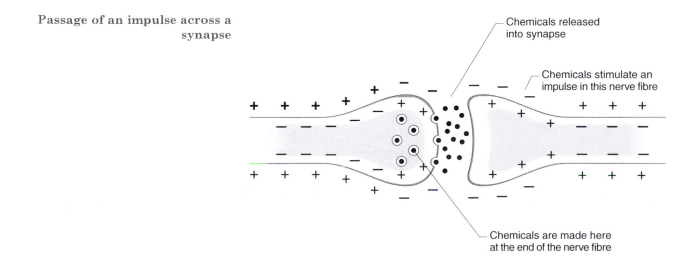

Chemicals released into synapse

Chemicals stimulate an impulse in this nerve fibre

Chemicals are made here at the end of the nerve fibre

being taken up by an adjacent neurone. This action causes an electrical impulse within the neurone.

From neurone to muscle fibre

As the motor nerve enters the muscle at the motor point, the individual neurones of that nerve branch off so that each neurone makes contact with the individual muscle cells. Motor neurones release a chemical transmitter into the muscle that causes all the muscle fibres in its **motor unit** to contract.

Technical note

The area of contact between the neurone and the muscle fibre is called the **neuromuscular junction** or **motor end plate**.

Synapse and neuromuscular junction

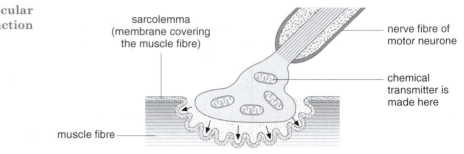

Voluntary or reflex

The CNS is involved in both reflex and voluntary actions. Voluntary actions, those which we can control such as speaking and walking, are initiated by the brain. A reflex response is a quick involuntary response to stimuli such as a hot plate. In reflex actions, impulses are passed through the sensory nerve fibres to the spinal cord and are then transmitted through relay neurones to motor neurones. This is called a spinal reflex. The message is also passed to the brain (as a result of impulses passing up the spinal cord) and you become aware of what you have done which often causes a vocal response!

Autonomic nervous system

The autonomic nervous system controls the involuntary activities of the smooth muscle, cardiac muscle and the glands. It is responsible for a variety of things from regulating the size of the pupil – vasodilation – and vasoconstriction – heart rate, gut movements and secretions from the glands.

There are two divisions within the autonomic system. The first is sympathetic, associated with stress, and the second, parasympathetic, associated with peace. Many organs receive a supply from both of these divisions – fibres from one division will stimulate an organ's fibres while fibres from the other division will inhibit it.

The sympathetic division is stimulated in periods of danger or stress and prepares the body for 'fight or flight'. This causes the heart rate to speed up, the pupils to dilate, sweating to increase, the bronchioles in the lungs to dilate and blood sugar levels to rise, as the blood flow through the muscles is increased. The parasympathetic division is stimulated in times of relaxation. These fibres stimulate digestion and absorption of food.

Effects of massage on the nerves

Tip

If the massage pressure is too light, it can become irritating. If the pressure is too deep, it can be painful

Massage can either have a stimulating or relaxing effect on local nerves depending on the movements carried out, for example effleurage can lead to the person calming down through slow, deep manipulation being applied or invigorated by applying brisk, superficial manipulations. Applying pressure to any painful areas, especially around the neck and shoulder region, will lead to temporary numbing and, as a result, pain relief.

The digestive system

The long muscular tube running all the way from the mouth to the anus is called the alimentary tract and is where digestion takes place. Food is taken in by mouth,

The digestive system

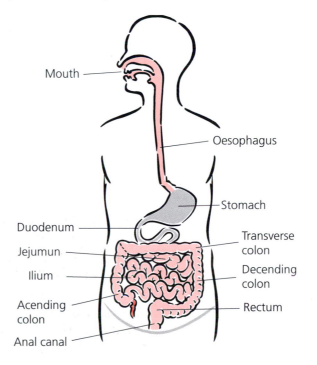

Mouth

Oesophagus

Stomach

Duodenum

Jejumun

Ilium

Acending colon

Anal canal

Transverse colon

Decending colon

Rectum

broken down and absorbed into the blood. Waste is then eliminated.

Structure

The digestive system comprises the following parts.

Mouth

In the mouth, food is broken down into smaller pieces by chewing and mixed with saliva from salivary glands. The enzyme ptyglin is contained in the saliva which works on some of the carbohydrates to turn them into smaller molecules of maltose and glucose.

Pharynx and oesophagus

The bolus of food is pushed to the back of the mouth where the pharynx muscles push it down into the oesophagus. The oesophagus is a long thin tube which leads to the stomach. The bolus moves through the oesophagus by peristalsis, muscle contractions which move food through the tract. We have no conscious control over this muscular action.

Stomach

This is a muscular organ situated on the left side of the abdomen below the diaphragm. In the stomach, food is broken down further, as it mixes with gastric juices and enzymes. Food can stay in the stomach for up to five hours until it turns into a liquid form, chyme. A hormone called gastrin stimulates the cells of the stomach to release hydrochloric acid. This reacts with the enzyme pepsin which helps break the food down further into peptones. Mucous secretion prevents the stomach from being damaged by the gastrin and acid production. At this point it goes into the small intestine.

Small intestine

This is about 8 metres long in total and consists of the duodenum, jejunum and the ileum. Peristalsis continues to help the food move along. Food is further digested with the aid of several juices. These are:

- **bile** produced in the liver and stored in the gall bladder, bile helps to break up fat droplets, a process known as **emulsification**, and neutralise the chyme

- **pancreatic juice** produced in the pancreas, this contains enzymes that continue to digest the fats, carbohydrates and proteins
- **intestinal juice** released by the small intestine, this completes the breakdown of all the nutrients.

From the duodenum, digested food enters the jejunum and ileum. The jejunum absorbs the nutritional elements within the food.

In the ileum there are thousands of minute villi that enable the digested food to be absorbed into the blood stream. From the small intestine, the food passes into the large intestine.

Absorption of food

Digested food is absorbed by diffusion through the villi of the small intestine. Simple sugars from digested carbohydrates and amino acids from protein pass from the villi and are carried to the liver where they are processed. Vitamins and minerals travel through the villi and are absorbed in the blood stream to help with the body's normal functions and cell metabolism. Fat molecules from digested fat pass into the intestinal lymphatics and are carried through the lymphatic circulation before they go into the blood and circulate.

The liver

The liver sits on the right side of the abdominal cavity under the diaphragm. It is the largest gland in the body and plays a major part in metabolism by regulating the absorption of nutrients from the small intestine.

The liver:

- secretes bile
- regulates blood sugar, amino acids, fat content and plasma proteins
- detoxifies waste and drugs
- stores vitamins A, D, E, K and B12 as well as minerals, iron, potassium and copper.

When the blood stream has absorbed the nutrients, it transports them to the cells in the body for metabolism. Glucose is used to provide energy for the body's cells. Amino acids are used to provide new tissue and repair any damaged cells. Fatty acids are use to produce heat and energy and some of the fats are used as a layer around vital organs such as the heart. Other fats are stored under the skin.

Large intestine

This is about 1.3 metres long and consists of the ascending, transverse and descending colons all of which are coiled around the small intestine. The large intestine divides into the **caecum**, **rectum** and **anal canal**. The caecum is where the appendix is attached and the ileum opens. The rectum, is a smaller muscular tube which runs through the pelvis and anal canal to its opening where solid waste matter from the body is excreted. This is part of the descending colon.

The functions of the large intestine are:

- absorption of water from the waste
- the making of waste (bacteria and food that is not digested)
- storage of waste
- elimination of waste through the anus to the outside of the body.

Tip

Never massage the abdomen after the client has just eaten or if there is any pain present

Effects of massage on the abdominal organs

Massaging the alimentary tract can aid peristalsis and help treat constipation.

Nutrition

A good nutritious diet is a major requirement for providing the body with energy, and the ability to grow, repair and maintain itself.

The five main groups of nutrients are:

1 carbohydrates
2 fats
3 proteins
4 minerals
5 vitamins

Water is also essential to the diet. Insufficient water intake leads to dehydration and constipation.

Carbohydrates

Carbohydrates are the main source of energy for the body. Excess carbohydrate is converted into fat, and most of it is stored as adipose tissue beneath the skin. There are three types of carbohydrates:

1   monosaccharides which are simple sugars
   - glucose   found in fruit, the blood of living animals and plant juices
   - fructose   found in fruits, plant juices and honey
   - galactose   found in the milk of mammals

2   disaccharides which are double sugars and are made of two monosaccharide units joined together
   - sucrose   found in sugar cane
   - sugar beet   found in fruits and carrots
   - maltose   formed during digestion of starch
   - lactose   found only in milk

3   polysaccharides which are formed from a varying number of monosaccharide units. They are divided into two groups
   - starches   found in cereals, pulses, root vegetables, bread, potatoes, pasta and rice
   - glycogen   made from glucose by animals, small amounts are stored in the liver and muscles for energy

Fibre

Fibre is a source of carbohydrate that we cannot digest. Fibre helps to keep the digestive system healthy. Fibre is found in all vegetable sources and whole grain cereals such as wheat, rice, oats, wholemeal bread, breakfast cereals and bran. Many fruits especially apples and plums are good sources. Food that is high in fibre contains more bulk but fewer calories. Fibre is made up of non-starch polysaccharides which can be either soluble or insoluble. Insoluble fibre helps food move through the digestive system by giving the muscles something to grip onto, therefore preventing constipation. An example is cellulose. Soluble fibre can help reduce the amount of cholesterol in the blood. Pectin is an example and is derived from apples, plums, turnips and sweet potatoes.

Fats

Fat provides energy in a concentrated form. It provides us with energy, warmth, and protects the vital organs such as the heart. Excess fat is stored in adipose tissue beneath the skin, and this gives the shape and contour of the body. Sources of fat in the diet are butter, margarine, oils, nuts, cream, egg yolk, cheese, lard and meats. Fatty foods are a source of the fat soluble vitamins A, D, E and K. They also supply essential fatty acids. Fatty acids may be saturated or unsaturated. Saturated fats are hard fats such as butter, lard and suet (animal sources). Unsaturated fats are vegetable oils such as corn, soya and sunflower.

Proteins

Protein is essential for major growth, repair, and maintenance of the body. It is a major constituent of all cells and forms antibodies, hormones and enzymes. Proteins are complex molecules that contain the elements carbon, hydrogen, oxygen, nitrogen and sometimes sulphur. Proteins form chains of amino acids which are linked. There are about 20 amino acids found in proteins, of which nine are termed essential.

- animal protein – contains all essential acids. These include meat, fish, milk, cheese and eggs.
- vegetable proteins – a few essential acids are missing from these. Food sources are cereals, pulses, nuts, vegetables and soya.

Protein is essential for growing children, adolescents, pregnant women, and people recovering from sickness.

Minerals

There are about 15 elements required by the body and these must be obtained from food. Major minerals are required in small amounts and they are:

- calcium
- phosphorus
- magnesium
- iron
- sodium and chlorine
- potassium
- zinc.

Vitamins

Vitamins are a group of chemical compounds that are required by the body in very small amounts. These should be obtained from food. Lack of vitamins will result in specific deficiency diseases. Vitamins are either fat soluble – A, D, E and K – or water soluble – B group, C

The respiratory and olfactory systems

Respiration is the process by which we inhale oxygen and exhale carbon dioxide, which is a waste product of oxidation. The primary organ used in respiration is the lungs.

Respiratory system

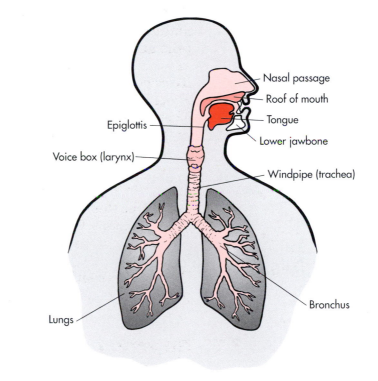

Nasal passage
Roof of mouth
Tongue
Epiglottis
Lower jawbone
Voice box (larynx)
Windpipe (trachea)
Bronchus
Lungs

When we breathe, we can breathe in through either the mouth or the nose. Breathing is more effective through the nose because it warms and moistens (with mucus) the air, filters dirt and dust (with the cilia) and alerts us to any potential problems of air quality by the sense of smell.

There are three types of breathing:

1   *Apical (shallow) breathing*
    This occurs when a person is excited, stressed or in danger. It only uses the upper lobe of the lung resulting in shallow breathing.

2   *Lateral costal breathing*
    This is deep, slow breathing which uses the upper and
    middle lobes of the lungs

3   *Diaphragmatic breathing*
    This type of breathing uses the upper, middle and lower
    lobes of the lungs. It is very deep and calming and is
    practised by people who play wind instruments.

The nose plays an important part in the olfactory system.
Sensory receptors attached to the first cranial or olfactory
nerve are present in the upper nasal passage. They are
coated with a watery mucus in which certain chemicals
dissolve. These then stimulate the sensory receptors and a
message is transmitted to the brain's olfactory bulb where
the smell is interpreted.

Olfactory ststem

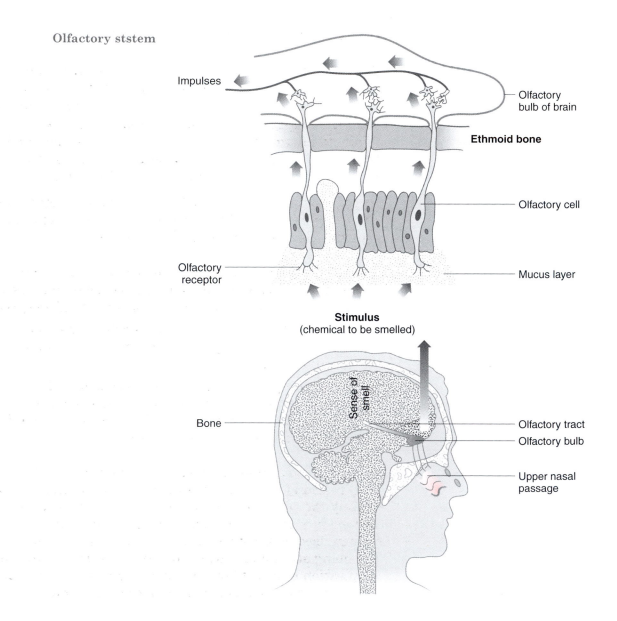

Smells can alter a person's mood and influence their behaviour. A good example of this are the animal pheromones which encourage sexual attention. The part of the brain involved in olfaction is very close to the areas of the brain which control emotions, the limbic system. In addition to being absorbed into the bloodstream, essential oils used in aromatherapy takes advantage of the limbic responses through olfaction.

The limbic system is the part of the brain that receives messages from the olfactory cells in the nose. It is involved in our emotions and consists of a group of structures that encircle the brainstem. Smells evoke feelings and may take on emotional significance through memory and association. This can be especially important in aromatherapy massage.

The breathing mechanism

At each intake of breath, the **intercostal muscles** situated between the ribs contract: this raises the rib cage and creates a greater space in the thoracic cavity. At the same time the diaphragm contracts and is pulled down, causing air to be drawn into the lungs. As the diaphragm and intercostal muscles relax and return to their original positions, the air is then pushed out of the lungs.

Respiration refers not only to breathing, but signifies the uptake of oxygen and production and removal of carbon dioxide. This takes place in three contexts:

1   An exchange between the air (from the external environment) and the blood. This exchange takes place in the lungs and is referred to as **external respiration**.
2   An exchange between the blood cells. This occurs throughout the body and is referred to as **internal respiration**.
3   An exchange within the cells of the body, where oxygen is used to 'burn' foodstuffs, releasing energy or synthesising cell materials. This occurs in the body and is referred to as **cellular respiration**.

During a body massage treatment, the rate of external respiration slows down to an even, easy rhythm. It involves mainly the thoracic region of the body, with only very small movements of the intercostal muscles. Internal respiration is increased slightly because the blood and lymph systems are being stimulated to rid the body of toxic waste. Cellular respiration occurs when the body's energies are not needed to carry out physical or mental activities. Some of this energy is used up by the normal functioning of the cell; the remainder is lost as heat, hence the feeling of warmth often associated with massage treatments.

Effects of massage on the respiratory system

Certain massage movements, for example tapotement and percussion, affect the lung tissue. Circulation to the bronchioles is increased which in turn nourishes and feeds the tissues. This improves both the elasticity of the lung tissue and gaseous exchange within the lungs.

It is important to encourage clients to breathe correctly, especially during treatments. Correct breathing can:

- help to prevent lung infections by increasing resistance
- help to improve lung elasticity
- encourage good posture
- help to maintain nutrient supply to muscles
- aid relaxation.

Tip

Never massage if the client has any acute respiratory conditions e.g. bronchitis.

The renal system

The renal system, or urinary system as it is sometimes known, deals with the elimination of liquid waste from the body. The urinary system is made up of:

- **two kidneys** these lie on either side of the spine at the bottom of the thoracic region and the top of the lumbar region. They filter the impurities from the blood, regulate the salt and water balance, maintain pH balance, produce urine and control fluid balance.
- **two ureters** these are two thin tubes which take the urine from the kidneys to the bladder.
- **the bladder** this is a pear shaped bag which is located in the pelvis. Urine is collected and stored here until ready to be released. Its size varies depending on how full or empty it is.
- **urethra** this takes the urine from the bladder to the outside of body. The urethra is longer in males than females.

right kidney · left kidney · ureter · urethra · bladder

Renal system

Effects of massage on the renal system

During massage, the lymphatic system is stimulated. This can increase the urine content passing to the bladder.

The endocrine system

Endocrine glands secrete hormones (chemical messengers) into the blood stream. They are then circulated around the body affecting their target organs. Most hormones are associated with long term changes, like the growth hormone, but some bring about fast changes, for instance the adrenaline which prepares the body very quickly when it is suddenly stressed.

Table 2.13 Endocrine glands and their functions

Gland	Hormone	Function
pituitary gland	follicle stimulating hormone (FSH) luteinizing hormone (LH) anti-diuretic hormone (ADH)	controls reproduction, affects the water balance, situated in the brain, the pituitary gland is also known as the Master gland because it secretes trophic hormones which act on other endocrine glands
pineal		affects growth and also development of sex glands
thyroid gland	thyroxine	controls rate of metabolism
thymus		helps immune system
parathyroid gland	parathormone	controls the blood calcium levels
pancreas	insulin	controls the blood sugar level
adrenal glands	adrenalin (medulla) glucocorticoids (cortex)	prepares the body for action reduces stress responses such as inflammation
	aldosterone (cortex)	controls potassium and sodium levels in the blood. This hormone can also cause excess oedema (water retention).
	corticosteroids (cortex)	help to maintain homeostasis
ovaries	oestrogen and progesterone	control development and function of female sex organs and associated sexual characteristics, e.g. fat being stored in the breasts, hips and thighs
testes	testosterone/androgens	control development and function of male sex organs and associated sexual characteristics, e.g. development of facial and body hair, muscular development

The endocrine system maintains homeostasis or constancy within the body. It can do this because the amount of hormone released by the endocrine glands is controlled by the amount of a particular hormone which is needed.

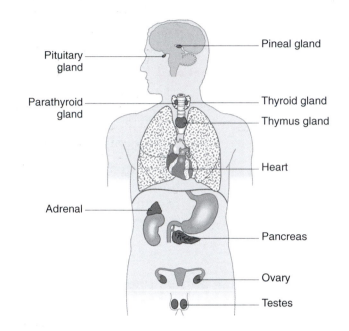

Pituitary gland

Pineal gland

Parathyroid gland

Thyroid gland

Thymus gland

Heart

Adrenal

Pancreas

Ovary

Testes

Glands of the endocrine system

Effects of massage on the endocrine system

High stress levels can affect the homeostasis of the body as well as being the root cause for a number of common illnesses such as headaches, digestive problems, high blood pressure and insomnia. Massage can help regulate the body by promoting relaxation which enables the body to function properly. Certain essential oils used in aromatherapy can also effect certain endocrine glands.

The breasts

The breasts are attached to a layer of connective tissue, and strands of connective tissue (suspensory ligaments) run through the breast tissue, attaching the skin to the connective tissue layer that covers the muscles. The hormone oestrogen is responsible for their growth during puberty. The breasts lie over the pectoral and serratus muscles.

The breasts are also known as the mammary glands and their main function is to produce milk after pregnancy (the hormone progesterone causes them to grow when pregnant). Milk is produced by the hormone prolactin and is passed through ducts to the nipple. Milk is then released during breast feeding, when the hormone oxytocin is produced as the baby starts to suckle. Oxytocin helps the uterus return to its normal size more quickly after birth, as it also causes the uterus to contract; therefore, breast feeding is beneficial in helping this to happen.

The glandular tissue that the breasts are composed of is very similar to the tissue found in the sweat glands. The cells that secrete the milk are supported by connective tissue and are divided into lobules that are separated by fat (adipose tissue): it is the fat that determines the size of the breast.

Breast tissue

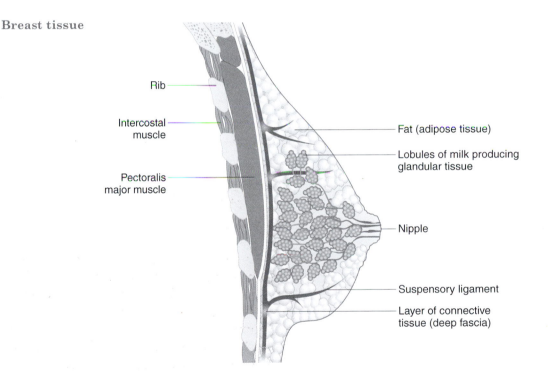

Rib

Intercostal muscle

Pectoralis major muscle

Fat (adipose tissue)

Lobules of milk producing glandular tissue

Nipple

Suspensory ligament

Layer of connective tissue (deep fascia)

The breasts contain

- **lymphatic vessels** – drainage takes place mainly at the axilla glands (situated under the arm)
- **blood vessels** – the main ones are the axillary and subclavian arteries
- **internal mammary nodes** – when the breasts are feeding these nerves are stimulated, the flow of oxytocin is stimulated which will promote the flow of milk.

Blood and lymph supply to the
breast area

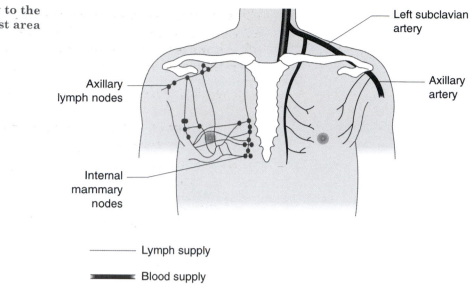

Psychological benefits

From headaches and insomnia, to digestive problems, high
blood pressure and depression, many common illnesses can
in some instances be stress related. Stress can also depress
the body's immune system making it more vulnerable to a
number of infections.

However, not all stress is negative. In the right amounts
and under the right circumstances it can be very positive.
Taking on a new challenge makes life exciting. Everyone
has their own stress threshold and a point when challenges
and everyday living become too much to cope with. If too
much physical or psychological strain is put upon us, the
normal balances of the body become upset. Combined with
other factors such as poor diet and lack of sleep, stress
levels can rocket and the results can vary enormously. High
blood pressure, migraine, sleeping problems, digestive
problems, minor aches and pains, depression, lack of
concentration, feeling constantly angry or irritable and skin
conditions such as eczema are just some of the conditions
that can be caused or brought on by stress.

Massage has long been used as a method of counteracting
stress and in today's world, stress is becoming increasingly
common. Massage helps to reeducate the body on how to
rest and relax. By rebalancing the body and boosting the
immune system, the body should be able to fight off
infection and get back on the road of recovery.

A relaxing massage can occasionally induce the client to fall
asleep. Most tend to fall into a state of deep relaxation.

Clients often feel more refreshed after a massage than after a full night's sleep. It is quite common for a client to return after a massage and announce they had slept much better than they had done for a long time.

The soothing effect of massage encourages:

- an improvement in concentration and alertness due to the increased oxygen to the brain
- emotional honesty as the client relaxes and tension is alleviated
- an increase in confidence brought about by physical touch and the uplifting effect of the massage
- an increase in energy levels brought about by the release of tension.

Knowledge review – anatomy, physiology and the effects of massage

1   Draw a large labelled diagram to show the structure of the skin. Include the following:
- 5 layers of the epidermis
- a hair follicle
- sweat and sebaceous glands
- nerve endings
- capillaries

2   Which structures are found beneath the dermis?

3   State two effects of massage on the skin.

4   Describe the endocrine system.

5   What effects does massage have on the endocrine system?

6   Name the three main types of blood vessels.

7   Which type of veins have valves and why?

8   Describe two effects of massage on the circulatory system.

9   Why do the cells in the body need a blood supply?

10   Name the lymphatic nodes on the diagram.

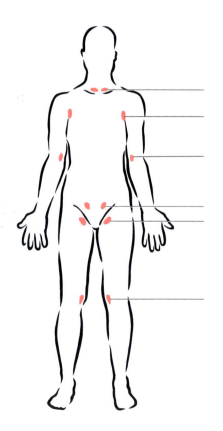

Lymphatic

11   Describe the main functions of the lymphatic system.

12   State the effect of massage on lymphatic circulation.

13   Label the organs of the digestive system diagram.

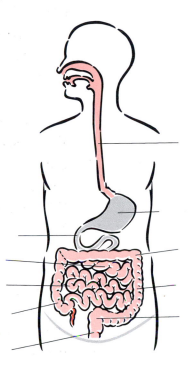

Digestive

14   What is the effect of massaging the alimentary tract?

15   Label the following diagram on the renal system.

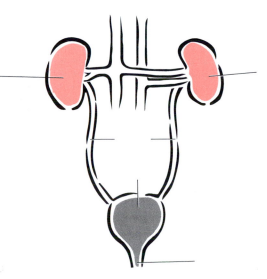

Renal

16   What is the main effect of massage on the renal system?

17   Label the muscles in the diagram of the abdominals.

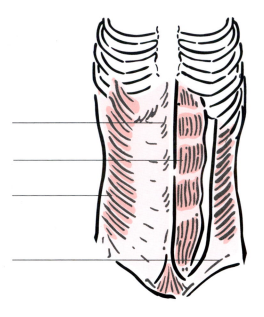

Abdominal

18   In which areas of the body would you find the following
● metatarsals
● metacarpals
● cervical vertebrae
● humerus
● tibia
● radius
● clavicle

19   State any effects of massage on the bones.

20   In what areas of the body would you find the following muscles and state the main function of each.
● trapezius
● pectoralis major
● deltoid
● tibialis anterior
● gastrocnemius
● quadriceps
● gluteals
● external oblique

21   Describe two effects massage has on muscles.

22 Describe the difference between a tendon and a ligament.

23 Describe the difference between voluntary and involuntary muscle tissue.

24 What is the function of connective tissue?

25 Describe the function of a sensory nerve.

26 Explain the effect of effleurage movement on the nerves.

27 Describe the type of joint found in the
- hip
- elbow
- knee

28 Describe the effect of massage on the joints.

29 What is an erythema and what are its possible causes?

30 What is the function of the olfactory system?

31 What are the benefits of breathing correctly?

32 State the effect massage has on the respiratory system.

Client consultation and contraindications to treatment

3

Learning objectives

This chapter covers the following:

- **client consultation**

- **contraindications**

- **figure diagnosis**

- **keeping records**

- **evaluating treatment**

This chapter explains the importance of and techniques required for client consultation and details the areas which must be covered and recorded on the client's records prior to commencing a massage treatment. It highlights the range of contraindications which could prevent or affect treatment.

Client consultation

Before commencing a massage treatment, the therapist needs to gain a range of information from the client. If the client has not been treated by you or one of your colleagues relatively recently, you should carry out a full consultation. During this consultation, a detailed record card must be completed, and it is essential that all personal details are recorded. If they are a regular client, you should begin each treatment with a scaled-down consultation.

Consultation

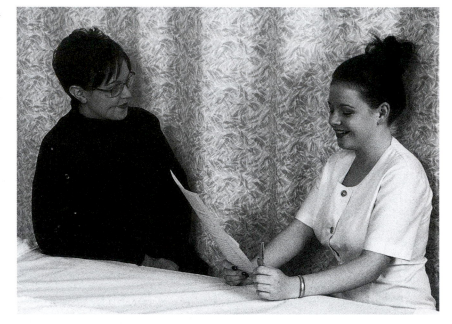

Tip

It is very important that you keep this record card up to date. Personal details need to be accurate and you should keep a log of any treatments given together with relevant notes.

Consultations should be carried out in a private area, for example, a treatment room or cubicle, as you will need to ask the client a series of questions, many of which may be of a personal or confidential nature like their medical history.

Aims of a consultation

The most important reason for carrying out a consultation is to ensure that the client is suitable for treatment and that they are not contraindicated in any way. As a therapist, it is essential that you are familiar with a whole range of conditions which contraindicate massage treatments. The most common are covered later in this chapter.

However, there are number of other things you should aim to achieve during the consultation process:

- put the client at ease
- build a good rapport with the client
- ascertain why the client has come for a massage. The client may have an underlying reason for seeking treatment which is not immediately obvious or which they are reluctant to admit, for example they may be suffering from stress, and you should try to identify this prior to commencing treatment
- build up knowledge about their lifestyle. You can do this by asking open questions
- ensure that the client has realistic expectations about the treatment
- ensure the treatment they have requested, or the one you have recommended, is the most suitable treatment for their needs.

Throughout the consultation, you should encourage the client to ask any questions which you should answer in a professional and honest manner. At the end of the consultation the client should understand everything that is going to take place and have an idea of what type of massage they will be receiving and what it involves. For example, if it comes to light that they have a lot of tension in the neck and shoulders you can spend more time in this area, or if they are menstruating, you can omit the abdomen area. Consultations also give the therapist an indication of any areas where the client does not want to be touched. At this stage, the client should be feeling relaxed and ready for their treatment.

If after the consultation you are unsure of the client's suitability for treatment, you should tactfully explain why it is important for them to seek permission from the doctor before treatment can be given.

Consultation form

An example of a consultation form follows. You can use the back to write treatment notes.

Client referral

A client may, after consultation, need to seek their doctor's approval in order for the treatment to be carried out. A

SALON NAME, ADDRESS, PHONE NUMBER

Part 1

Name: _____   Address: _____

Telephone number – Daytime: _____   Evening: _____   _____

Date of birth: _____   Occupation: _____   _____

Part 2: Medical history

Name of doctor: _____   Telephone number: _____

	Yes	No	
Any recent illness?	☐	☐	
Are you taking any medication at present?	☐	☐	If yes, what are you taking? _____
Are you receiving any medical treatment?	☐	☐	If yes, what treatment? _____

Part 3: Do you suffer from any of the following?

	Yes	No		Yes	No
Heart condition	☐	☐	Dysfunction or disorders to the nervous system	☐	☐
Epilepsy	☐	☐	Cancer	☐	☐
Circulatory problems	☐	☐	Recent operations/scar tissue	☐	☐
Thrombosis/phlebitis	☐	☐	Skin diseases or disorders	☐	☐
Diabetes	☐	☐	Any swellings or inflamed areas	☐	☐
High/low blood pressure	☐	☐	Fractures/recent sprains/muscle strains	☐	☐

Any other: _____

Part 4: Female questions only

Number of pregnancies: ____   Dates: _____   Could you be pregnant? ____   How many months _____

	Yes	No		Yes	No
Could you be menopausal?	☐	☐	Do you suffer from pre menstrual tension?	☐	☐
Are you menstruating at present?	☐	☐	Do you suffer from period problems?	☐	☐

Part 5: General

Do you suffer from any of the following?

	Yes	No	
Skin complaints e.g. psoriasis/allergies/eczema/dermatitis/other	☐	☐	
Muscles, joints conditions e.g. arthritis/rheumatism/muscular aches and pains/other	☐	☐	
Respiratory conditions e.g. asthma/sore throat/colds/other	☐	☐	
Digestive complaints e.g. indigestion/constipation/other	☐	☐	
Urinary problems e.g. fluid retention/water infection/thrush/other	☐	☐	
Do you suffer from migraine/headaches?	☐	☐	If so, how often? _____

Part 6: Overall summary of clients general health

_____

_____

Part 7: Summary

Is GP referral required? _____   GP approval received _____   Date: _____

Part 8: General lifestyle

Do you smoke? ____   If yes, approx how many per day? _____   On average, how many units of alcohol do you consume per week? _____

How many cups of tea/coffee do you drink per day? _____

Generally, how would you describe your diet? _____   What are you hobbies? _____

Do you take any vitamin or other supplements? _____   How do you relax? _____

Do you exercise on a regular basis? _____   What is your general sleep pattern? _____

If yes, what type of exercise? _____   How often? _____   On average, how many hours do you sleep per night? _____

How would you describe your energy levels?   low ☐   medium ☐   high ☐

At the moment are you feeling: anxious ☐   deperssed ☐   stressed ☐

Client declaration

The information I have given is correct, and I am therefore willing to proceed with the treatment that has been discussed.

Treatment agreed: _____

Client signature: _____   Date: _____   Therapist signature: _____

A consultation form

simple and easy way of getting approval without disturbing the doctor too much is to compose a simple standard letter for which only the doctor's signature is required.

Sample doctor's approval letter

Date

Clinic address

Dear Dr Jones

A patient of yours, Jenny Smith, has requested a body massage treatment.

After carrying out a consultation I learned that she is suffering from epilepsy.

I would, therefore, be very grateful if you would indicate by signing the attached, if you think Jenny is suitable for treatment.

Many Thanks,

Therapist

Adele O'Keefe

Tip

Don't forget, if you keep your records on computer, you must observe the Data Protection Act 1984 explained in Chapter 1.

Tip

Dealing with several clients one after another can be very exhausting. Try to 'switch off' between each one. This will help you feel less tired at the end of the day. Listen, but remember not to take on your clients' problems or you will become emotionally and physically drained!

Consent form

The above treatment you have requested, is suitable/unsuitable for the above named client.

Signed:

Dr Jones

Date:

Once the form has been completed, it is extremely important to get the client to sign it. This indicates proof of accuracy. It the client fails to divulge any information, for example a heart condition, you have the evidence that these questions were asked and the fact that you were unaware of this condition was not a result of negligence. Whenever you treat a client, you should also sign the card on which the treatment has been noted. In a multi-therapist practice, it will then be clear which therapist performed which treatments.

Contraindications

One of the key things to identify during a client consultation are any conditions that contraindicate the proposed treatment. A contraindication is any condition or symptom of the body that prevents a treatment taking place. It is very important that you have a good knowledge of all contraindications to body massage before carrying out a treatment. It is essential that you check thoroughly for these at the consultation as inappropriate treatment could incur risk to the client, therapist and other clients through cross-infection.

Contraindications can be either local or general. A local contraindication is one in which the area surrounding the condition must be avoided, for example if there is a varicose vein on the calf muscle, you should avoid massaging the lower leg. A general contraindication is one in which on no account should the client be massaged. Only when the condition clears up or approval is given by the client's doctor in writing can the client receive treatment.

Local or restrictive contraindications

With local contraindications, although the affected areas should be avoided, other areas of the body can usually still be massaged. If you are in any doubt, refer your client to their GP for medical advice.

Avoid massaging over:

- cuts, bruises and recent scar tissue, less than 6 months old. As well as being painful, there is a risk of infection
- areas affected by skin disorders such as eczema, psoriasis and dermatitis
- skin abrasions – risk of infection
- areas affected by sunburn – painful
- bites and stings – as well as being painful, there is a risk of infection
- abdomen if the client is menstruating or in the early stages of pregnancy
- swellings – medical advice should be sought if the reason for an oedema is unclear
- severe varicose veins – massage can worsen this condition
- local areas affected by thrombosis. This condition is quite common in the deep veins of the calves. Blood

tends to clot in the veins and massage may disturb the clot causing it to start moving through the veins and end up causing a blockage in a major organ

- fractures and sprains
- acute joint conditions and tender muscles – unless medical advice has been sought
- areas of inflammation
- moles and warts
- areas of thin, crêpey skin – avoid deep manipulations and tapotement movements

Health & Safety

Never perform massage on a client whom you suspect is under the influence of alcohol or drugs. Also, do not perform treatments on a client suffering from fever, infectious diseases or who is feeling generally unwell.

General or total contraindications

If any of the following conditions are present, medical advice should always be sought prior to treatment. In many cases you will need to exercise special care if given the go-ahead for treatment.

- some long-term medication – check with the client's GP if you are unsure
- asthma – although massage can help alleviate symptoms, medical advice must be sought if the condition is severe
- undiagnosed lumps, bumps and swellings
- loss of skin sensation – medical advice must be sought
- cancer – massage should only be carried out on people suffering from cancer under medical supervision as it could cause the cancer cells to spread via the lymph.
- nervous disorders – medical advice must be sought
- embolism – medical advice must be sought
- spastic conditions – massage could worsen symptoms
- blood pressure problems
  - high blood pressure – medical approval will usually be given as massage can often help this condition
  - low blood pressure – this can lead to clients feeling faint or dizzy, so if medical permission is granted, you must ensure that the client is supervised when they get up off of the massage couch
- heart conditions – massage stimulates the circulation and this may have an effect on any heart condition. Always seek medical consent
- during the active phase of rheumatoid arthritis
- epilepsy – medical permission will usually be given for massage in cases of epilepsy, as in most cases this condition will be controlled with medication.

However, you should never leave an epileptic client unattended

- diabetes – many people with this condition are prone to circulation problems and also problems with skin sensation. Take special care when performing massage treatments.

Skin diseases and disorders

The skin is covered by micro-organisms which cannot be seen by the naked eye. Some of these micro-organisms are responsible for some of the skin diseases and disorders that you are likely to come across as you practice body massage. You need to be able to recognise at least the most common ones and understand which do and which do not contraindicate treatments. For those that contraindicate treatment, refer the client to their doctor, as there is a risk of cross-infection.

Micro-organisms can be pathogenic – disease-producing – or non-pathogenic. A non-pathogenic organism is not harmful. In fact many non-pathogenic organisms are beneficial and help contribute to our general health.

A **disease** is an infectious, transferable, pathogenic condition but a **disorder** is a non-infectious, non-pathogenic condition of the skin, hair or scalp. As a general rule, where skin disorders are present, if they contraindicate treatment in any way, it will be local rather that total. Referring or refusing to treat a client who clearly has a non-pathogenic disorder can cause them considerable anguish, while treating someone with an infectious disease can put you and your other clients at risk of cross-infection.

Skin diseases

An infectious disease can be passed on from one person to the other by air droplets, for example when coughing and sneezing. A contagious disease is passed on through direct or indirect contact for example touching the infected area or using materials that have touched it. A good example of how this can happen is when a towel touched by an infected person is reused.

There are four types of pathogenic micro-organisms:

1 bacteria
2 virus
3 fungus
4 infestations.

In this next section, we take a look at some of the most common skin diseases that would contraindicate treatment.

Bacteria

Bacteria are minute, unicellular micro-organisms. They are found almost everywhere and are either pathogenic or non-pathogenic.

Bacteria can enter the body in several ways through:

- direct contact, like touching an infected person
- unhygienic working practices, like the use of unsterilised equipment
- indirect contact, like touching contaminated objects
- consuming contaminated food
- respiration as many bacteria are airborne.

Table 3.1 *Common bacterial infections*

Condition	Status	Description
impetigo	highly contagious and infectious	An infection of the epidermis, most commonly found on the face where pus-filled blisters form. When burst, the infection spreads and yellow crusts are formed. Requires medical treatment
boils (furuncle)	infectious	an infection of the hair follicle caused by the staphylococci bacteria. It usually starts as a small red nodule and gradually increases in size simultaneously becoming inflamed and very painful
carbuncle	infectious	several boils appear together and these can be found almost anywhere on the body
conjunctivitis	infectious and contagious	inflammation of the lining of the eyelid and the mucous membrane that covers the eye. The eye becomes red, itchy and exudes pus. Avoid facial massage
styes	infectious	small pus-filled adhesions on the lash line resulting in an infected hair follicle. Avoid facial massage

Impetigo

Boils

As a therapist you must not provide treatment to anyone that has any visible signs of bacterial infection. Infections usually present themselves as pus, which is usually present in abscesses, boils and pustules.

Viruses

Viruses are smaller micro-organisms than bacteria. They are classed as parasites because they can only live and reproduce within living cells. They spread by multiplying within a healthy tissue cell until they burst the cell wall. They are then free to invade other cells and repeat the process, therefore spreading the infection.

Viruses are responsible for diseases as wide-ranging as influenza, chicken pox, measles, hepatitis B and AIDS (Acquired Immune Deficiency Syndrome), which is caused by HIV (Human Immunopathic Virus).

Table 3.2 *Common viral infections*

Condition	Status	Description	
herpes zoster (shingles)	infectious	Attacks the nerve pathways causing significant pain. Small blister-like spots on the skin's surface near the nerve endings. Found almost anywhere on the body.	
herpes simplex (cold sore)	infectious and contagious	Small blisters that burst forming an oozing crust, usually occurring around the mouth area. Usually triggered by changes in the temperature, ultraviolet light, ill health or stress-related illnesses	Herpes Simplex
warts	infectious and contagious	Common warts appear on the hands and face as a result of abnormal reproduction of the cells in the germinativum layer of the epidermis. Warts are infectious and should be referred to the doctor.	Warts
verrucae (plantar warts)	infectious and highly contagious	Found on the feet. Round and firm with a rough surface. Client should be referred to a chiropodist.	Verrucae

Fungi

Fungal diseases are spread by direct and indirect contact. Like viruses, they are classed as parasites. Moulds, yeasts and mildew are all fungi. They cannot manufacture their own food and therefore need to obtain food from other living organisms. A good example of this is ringworm.

Table 3.3 *Common fungal infections*

Ringworm

Condition	Status	Description
Ringworm	highly infectious and contagious	Starts as small red circular patches. Affects the skin on different parts of the body. Healing takes place from the centre, so appears as single or multiple-ringed lesions. The fungus produces enzymes which break down the keratin. These can appear as a mild scaling to more severe areas which are inflamed and extremely itchy. The small maculae – or flat spot – is red and tends to spread outwards
tinea pedis/ athletes foot	very contagious	The name given when ringworm affects the feet. The fungus is usually found in-between the toes and then tends to spread to the sides of the feet and the soles. Its appearance is usually flaking, cracking and weeping, accompanied by itchiness.
tinea unguium	infectious and contagious	The name given when ringworm affects the nails. The fungus usually invades the free edge and then spreads to the nail root. It can either appear as whitish patches which can be scraped off, or as yellow streaks which are in the middle of the nail. The nail plate becomes very spongy, and furrowed, and in some cases will become completely detached.
tinea corporis	infectious and contagious	The name given when ringworm affects the whole body. When it affects only the upper trunk it is known as tinea versicolor. Red pimples appear and spread at the edges, leaving a red ring with a normal skin colour in the middle. Pustules and scales usually develop over the rings.

Infestations

Infestations are tiny animal parasites that invade the skin and live off human blood. These are highly contagious.

Table 3.4 *Common infestations*

Condition	Status	Description
scabies	contagious	caused by a female mite which is fertilised on the skin's surface and then burrows into the skin to lay its eggs; this condition is often referred to as 'the itch'. The eggs hatch after four days, and ten days later the mature mite appears on the skin's surface. Scabies tends to invade in-between the fingers, on the palms and on the soles. They appear as grey-like ridges that track the routes of the burrows in the skin. The itch is a result of pimples caused by allergic reaction to the mite, its eggs and larvae. This gets worse as body temperature increases. Constant scratching produces inflammation and causes the skin to become coarser.
pediculosis capis (head lice)	extremely contagious by direct and indirect contact	caused by a small animal parasite that lives for approximately 30 days by sucking the blood from the scalp. The lice cling to the hair of the scalp and lay eggs attached to the hair close to the skin. Before laying eggs, lice first inject the site with an anticoagulant which causes irritation. The resultant scratching can cause secondary infection. Although lice lay up to 300 eggs in their lifetime, only a few survive and a typical infestation amounts to about 20 lice. Towels and bedding which have been in contact with this condition should be disinfected before being laundered.
pediculosis pubis	extremely contagious	a condition in which small parasites infest the body hair – usually the pubic hair, eyelashes and eyebrows. The lice cling to the hair of the body, eggs are laid, attached to the hair close to the skin. The lice bite the skin to suck out the blood for nourishment, creating an irritation and leaving small red marks. Itching can lead to secondary bacterial infection.
pediculosis corporis	very infectious and contagious	small parasites feed and live on the body skin. The lice cling to the hair of the body, eggs are laid, attached to the hair close to the skin. The lice bite the skin to suck out the blood for nourishment, creating an irritation and leaving small red marks. Itching can lead to secondary bacterial infection.

Scabies

Skin disorders

The following is a list of some of the most common skin disorders which you might encounter as a massage therapist. These skin conditions are neither infectious nor contagious. They can broadly be classified as skin conditions, malignant skin conditions, allergic conditions, pigmentation disorders and sebaceous gland disorders.

Skin conditions

Table 3.5 *Common skin conditions*

Condition	Description
psoriasis	normally affects the knees, lower back and scalp although it can also affect other areas of the body. Its appearance is red, itchy flaky skin. The red patches of skin are covered in waxy, silvery scales, and secondary infection can occur if bacteria enters skin broken through scratching. No treatment is completely effective, although medication can help relieve the symptoms. *This condition is not infectious and does not contraindicate treatment.* Psoriasis
seborrheic (senile) warts	warts are slightly raised, black or brown in colour, rough patches of skin. They are usually found on the trunk, scalp, and the temples and can be cauterised by a physician. *This condition is not infectious.*
verrucae filliforms (skin tags)	skin coloured threads of skin, found mainly on the eyelids and neck area, although they may occur on other areas such as the underarm region. *These are not infectious.*
xanthomas	found on the eyelids. Their appearance is a flat or raised area of skin which is yellow in colour. Their growth is thought to be connected with diabetes and abnormal blood pressure and can sometimes be corrected with a low fat diet. *They are not infectious and should not interfere with body massage treatments in any way.*
erythema	an area of the skin in which the blood vessels have dilated due to either injury or inflammation. The affected area appears red and erythema may occur locally or generally all over the skin. It is not infectious. The cause of the condition needs to be identified, as it may be an allergic reaction. If the cause is unknown, *the client should be referred to the doctor.*

Malignant skin conditions

Table 3.6 Malignant skin conditions

Condition	Description
squamous cell carcinomas or prickle cell cancers	can occur anywhere on the skin although it originates in the epidermis. When fully formed, the carcinoma appears as a raised area of skin. *This is a medical condition* and is often treated by radiation
basal cell carcinomas or rodent ulcers	usually occurs on the face and tends to occur in middle age. These tend to be small shiny waxy nodules with a depressed centre. The disease extends with more nodules appearing on the border of the original ulcer. *This is a medical condition*
Malignant melanomas/ moles	rapidly growing skin cancer. It is not infectious. If you notice that a client has a mole which is changing in size, structure or colour, bleeds or is itchy, you should recommend that they *seek medical advice* without causing alarm. Melanomas start as a bluish/black mole which starts to get bigger quite quickly, at the same time getting darker in colour and develops a halo of pigmentation around it. Later it becomes raised, ulcerates and bleeds. Secondary growths will develop in the internal organs if the melanoma is not treated. These are usually found on the lower abdomen, legs and feet.

Malignant melanoma

Allergic conditions

An allergic reaction appears as an irritation. The area is usually itchy, red and swollen accompanied by discomfort. The substance causing the reaction is referred to as an allergen. Allergens may be vegetable, animal or chemical substances and may be eaten, inhaled or absorbed following contact of the skin. Most allergens are proteins that are ingested or chemicals which come into contact with the skin's surface.

Every individual has a different tolerance to the various substances encountered in daily life. What may cause an allergic reaction to one person may well be perfectly harmless to another. You may suddenly become allergic to a substance that you have been using for years and equally you may also cease to be allergic to something to which you have always been allergic.

The type of allergens known to cause an allergic skin reaction are

- sticking plaster
- nail enamel

Tip

Some essential oils used in aromatherapy massage are contraindicated for certain conditions. If medical consent is given for massage for a client suffering from a certain condition, you should check to see if there are any contraindicated oils associated with that condition. See chapter 9.

- hair and lash dyes
- lanolin
- certain foods, especially peanuts, lobster, cow's milk and strawberries
- plants such as chrysanthemums
- metal objects containing nickel

The use of hypoallergenic body products minimises the risk of skin contact with any irritants.

A number of more specific conditions can result from allergies, see Table 3.7:

Table 3.7 *Allergic conditions*

Condition	Description	
dermatitis	there are two types of dermatitis: primary dermatitis is when the skin is irritated by the action of a substance on the skin which leads to skin inflammation and allergic dermatitis which occurs on exposure to a particular substance. The skin quickly becomes irritated, causing an allergic reaction. If the skin reacts to a skin irritant outside the body, the reaction is localised. Repeated contact with the allergen will lead to hypersensitivity. If the irritant gains entry into the body, it will be transported by the bloodstream and cause an overall allergic reaction. Dermatitis is not infectious, and the skin appears as red and swollen with the possibility of blisters. The treatment is to *avoid the substance*, use steroid creams to soothe the damaged skin and barrier cream to help avoid contact with the irritant(s).	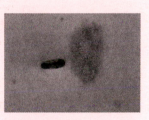 **Dermatitis** 
eczema	eczema normally occurs on the face and neck, and areas such as inner creases of the elbow and behind the knee area. The skin is usually red, swollen and blistered. The blisters leak tissue fluid which later hardens producing scabs. It is usually caused by skin contact either internally or externally with an irritant. Treatment is steroid cream. Special diets can help as can avoidance of the irritant.	 **Eczema**
Urticaria (nettle rash)	This is a minor skin disorder caused by contact with an allergen, either external such as insect bites or internal, such as food or drugs. The condition exhibits itself in raised, round whitish skin weals accompanied by erythema. The treatment is antihistamines to reduce the itching and avoidance of the allergen.	 **Urticaria**

Pigmentation disorders

Pigmentation of the skin tends to vary according to a person's genetic characteristics. Generally the darker the skin the more pigmentation is present. Abnormal changes in the skin can cause pigmentation to change. **Hypopigmentation** is loss of pigmentation in the skin. **Hyperpigmentation** is increased pigment production.

Table 3.8 Pigmentation conditions

Condition	Description
junction naevi	*non-infectious* and can appear anywhere on the body. They are harmless, localised collections of naevoid cells that arise from mass local production of pigment-forming cells. They tend to vary from brown colours to black
Vascular naevi	skin condition in which small or large areas of skin pigmentation are caused by the permanent dilation of blood capillaries
Spider naevi (stellate haemangiomas)	dilated blood vessels forming a star shape or spider pattern. These can occur on the cheek area, upper body, the arms and neck. It is usually caused by an injury to the skin and can be treated by diathermy.
dermal naevi	about 1cm wide, they appear smooth and dome shaped, their colour ranging from normal to a dark brown. Sometimes one or more hairs grow out of them and they are usually situated on the face.
cellular naevi (moles)	skin condition in which changes in the cells of the skin result in malformations.
hairy naevi	slightly raised moles that vary in size from about 3cm to much larger. Coarse hairs grow from the surface and colour ranges from fawn to dark brown. They can appear anywhere on the skin.
port wine stains	dilated capillaries appear in large areas and the naevus is flat and smooth. Usually found on the face and neck area. Camouflage creams are usually effective in disguising these.
Strawberry marks (naevi vasculosis)	red or purplish raised marks which appear from birth. These can be of any size and located anywhere on the skin. Concealing preparations may be used to cover the condition.
Chloasma (liver spots)	the result of increased skin pigmentation in specific areas of the body, the most common sites being upper chest, forearms, backs of hands, temples and the orehead. Their appearance is usually flat and smooth with an irregular shape. Colour ranges from light tan to dark brown. They often occur during pregnancy and can also be the result of taking the contraceptive pill, as oestrogen (female hormone) is thought to stimulate melanin production. Chloasma is best kept out of the sun, as the condition will worsen.

Spider Naevus

Strawberry Naevus

Table 3.8 *(continued)*

Condition	Description	
vitiligo (leucoderma)	characterised by areas of the skin that have lost their pigmentation and are completely white in colour. Their appearance is symmetrically shaped patches of skin, usually situated on the thigh, lower abdomen, face and neck. If vitiligo occurs over hairy areas like eyebrows, the hairs will also lose their pigmentation. Avoid ultraviolet light as the skin does not have the same protection.	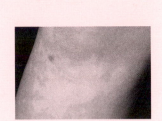 Vitiligo
albinism	skin cannot produce the melanin pigment, therefore the hair and skin lack colour. The skin tends to be very pink, the eyes are pink and extremely sensitive to light, and the hair is white. This condition can occur on the entire skin. The skin should not be exposed to ultraviolet light, and sunglasses should be worn to protect the eyes.	

A naevus is any abnormal skin pigmentation. None of these conditions are infectious.

Sebaceous gland disorders

Table 3.9 *Sebaceous gland disorders*

Condition	Description	
Acne rosacea	tends to occur at puberty, when the hormone imbalance in the body influences the activity of the sebaceous glands, causing an increased production of sebum. The sebum may stay in the sebaceous ducts, causing congestion and bacterial infection of the surrounding tissue. The skin tends to be inflamed accompanied by comedones (blackheads), pustules and papules (pimples). These are usually situated on the face area, but can occur on the chest and back. The client must be referred to seek medical advice.	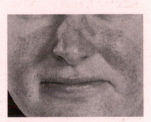 Acne rosacea
sebaceous cysts, steatomas or wens	tend to be semi-globular in shape, either raised or flat, hard or soft. The cysts can be the same colour as the skin, or red if there is a secondary bacterial infection. Sacs of sebum which form in the hair follicles or under the sebaceous glands in the skin: the sebum becomes blocked, the sebaceous gland becomes distended and a lump forms. Can form anywhere on the skin, and medical advice should be sought by the client.	
seborrhoea	excessive secretion of sebum from the sebaceous glands. Tends to occur in puberty, as a result of the hormonal changes that occur. The skin appears coarse and greasy, comedones, pustules and papules are present. This condition tends to affect the scalp and face, but sometimes also the back and chest area. Medical advice may be sought.	

Figure diagnosis

Once all relevant personal details have been completed and any contraindications ruled out, you should undertake a body analysis. It is extremely important to analyse the posture and figure of the client as part of the consultation, to ensure the treatments recommended are going to suit the client's requirements and are going to be the most effective.

There are a number of so-called figure faults. The most common condition found in female clients is a pear-shaped figure which is characterised by:

- heavy buttocks and thighs
- protruding abdomen
- round shoulders
- a large chest which can sometimes lead to round shoulders.

Many figure faults are due to slack muscles which can be caused by lack of exercise, pregnancy, illness or a sedentary life style.

Mesomorph

Body types

There are three main body types which you should learn to recognise as a therapist – endomorph, ectomorph and mesomorph. Being able to recognise these types will help you to distinguish between figure faults which can be changed by posture, diet and exercise and hereditary shapes which by and large will remain the same regardless of posture and diet.

Endomorph

Endomorph

This type tends to have a higher proportion of fat to muscle. Endomorphs tend to put on weight very easily. Fat deposits around the abdomen, thighs, hips and the shoulders. The hands and feet tend to be small and the neck and limbs short.

Ectomorph

This type tends to be lean and angular with small joints and long limbs. There is practically no body fat or muscle bulk and ectomorphs do not easily gain weight.

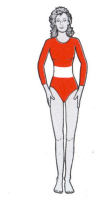

Ectomorph

Mesomorph

These are athletic body types who tend not to have any weight problems. Mesomorphs tend to have broad shoulders and well-toned muscles with an even distribution of weight.

Being able to diagnose figure type enables you to adapt the massage technique as appropriate. It also enables you to recommend postural exercises to clients who have postural conditions and can be helped in this way. In some instances, you may be the first person to recognise a fault that potentially requires medical attention.

It is important to be able to accurately diagnose figure faults, as incorrect exercises could make a postural condition worse. Very often it is habitual bad posture that creates the postural defects and the use of corrective exercises will eventually improve the condition in most cases. Some people are born with excellent postures, but for those who are not, it can be learnt. Professional models usually elegantly glide along. They practice until it becomes second nature. Good posture is the co-ordination and interplay of the extensor and flexor muscles of the body. If one group of muscles become weaker or stronger, the whole postural balance gets out of balance. Bad posture not only looks unattractive but can also bring about postural defects.

Tip

Don't forget your posture when you are working.

Carrying out the assessment

The initial figure assessment is visual. It is easy to assess the figure shape even when the client is fully dressed. The next stage is to ask the client to remove their clothes down to the underwear. It is best to check for posture and figure faults in front of a full length mirror. In this way, the client can observe how their posture may be corrected. Ensure that you observe the client from the front, the back and both sides.

Inspection from the front

A client who has good posture will stand tall and straight with their weight evenly distributed on both legs. Look for the following:

1   The head should be level, the chin tucked in and the ears level and even.
2   The shoulders should be level, slightly back with the chest and thorax broad and out.

Assessing posture

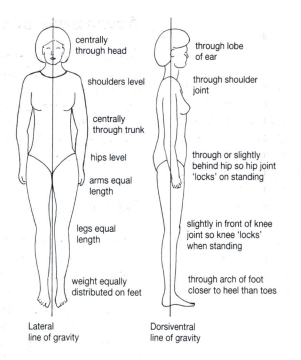

centrally
through head

shoulders level

centrally
through trunk

hips level

arms equal
length

legs equal
length

weight equally
distributed on feet

Lateral
line of gravity

through lobe
of ear

through shoulder
joint

through or slightly
behind hip so hip joint
'locks' on standing

slightly in front of knee
joint so knee 'locks'
when standing

through arch of foot
closer to heel than toes

Dorsiventral
line of gravity

Tip

Remember whilst some postural disorders are because of bad posture others are generic postural deformities which cannot be corrected or remedied.

3   The arms and hands should be relaxed and down by the sides of the thigh but not too far forward.

4   The waist should be evenly curved and not more apparent on one side than the other, with hips level not one higher up than the other.

5   The abdomen muscles should be slightly retracted.

6   The legs and knees should be straight, not tightly braced, feet facing forwards, slightly apart and flat feet, knock knees and bandy legs should be noted.

Inspection from the back

1   Check the head, ears and shoulders again from the back view looking out for the same things as before.

2   The medial borders of the scapula should be an even distance from the spine. The inferior angles of the scapula should be lying flat and level against the back of the chest wall.

3   Check the waist and hips as before.

4   Check that the spine is straight down the back and not curved in either direction.

5   Check the gluteal folds are even and at the same height.

6   Inspect the legs and feet again as before.

Tip

One shoulder being lower than the other in women can be a result of carrying heavy bags on the same side of the body. The dropped or lower shoulder develops shortened muscles which cause the opposite side of the body to compensate and its muscles to lengthen. The waist will also form an uneven curve.

Technical tip

The pelvic floor muscles help with excretion and support the organs in the abdomen and pelvis.

Advantages of good posture

Good posture enables more effective breathing, as the chest is not contracted, and more efficient functioning of the digestive organs, as they are not compressed. Muscles will not become as tired if the body weight is evenly distributed, and when bones are in the correct position, postural defects do not occur. Good posture also makes a person's figure much better.

Treating poor posture

Poor posture can cause a slight scoliosis over a period of time. In treating this, the aim is to correct the general poor posture. An appropriate treatment for scoliosis would be static contractions, tensing or tightening muscles without changing their length. These could be given to the muscles of the neck and head, extensors of the back, abdominal muscles, extensors of the hip and knee and the small muscles in the feet in various positions such as lying, sitting and standing. Exercises involving co-ordination and balance should also be taught. Remember, holding the correct posture during the exercise is of great importance, not just the exercise itself. Each client will have individual requirements depending on their problem.

Common figure faults

The following are types of postural conditions that you may encounter as a massage therapist, and exercises to tackle them.

Figure faults

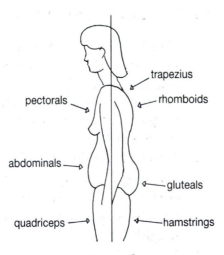

Table 3.10 Postural conditions

Condition   Exercise

flat back   characterised by the pelvis being tilted backwards, the lumbar region of the spine being flat and the hamstrings shortened. The client looks very square shouldered and erect as the curves of the spine are almost ironed. Mobility exercises help to mobilise and strengthen the spine and stretch the shortened muscles.

- hump and hollow the spine
- trunk movements, including forward bends, side flexions in the sitting position and rotations.

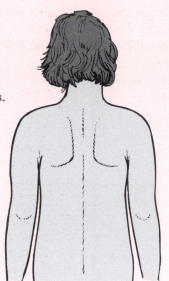

Flat back

pelvic tilt   characterised by the angle made between a horizontal line and a line drawn from the top of the sypmhesis pubis to the sacral promontory. If the pelvis tilts too far backwards the curve in the lumbar region can become flattened. If it tilts too far forwards, the lumbar vertabrae can become hyperextended

Note: The angle is greater in the female than in the male and also increases considerably during pregnancy as the ligaments relax and movement is increased

Lie on back, knees bent, arms relaxed at sides. Push the hollow of the back into the floor, hold and relax. Standing with feet slightly apart, knees bent, gently swing pelvis forward, if the tilt is too far backwards, or backwards, if the tilt is too far forward. Kneel on all fours and gently hump and hollow the back.

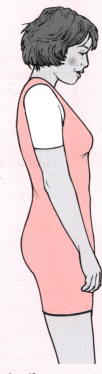

Pelvic tilt

Table 3.10 (continued)

Condition	Exercise
kyphosis (round shoulders)	usually, but not exclusively, caused by habitual bad posture kyphosis is characterised by an exaggeration of normal backward curve of the spine in the thoracic region. The client will have a poking chin and round shoulders. The pectoral muscles are tight and shortened with the upper back muscles overstretched and weak. This condition is often accompanied by lordosis. aim is to loosen the tightened structures and strengthen those which are stretched. Stand with feet slightly apart and shoulders relaxed, rotate the shoulders in a backwards direction. NB: Tight muscles can be stretched when massage is being performed by using the fingers or thumbs and kneading the smaller muscles, and on larger muscles using palmar kneading.

Kyphosis

lordosis (hollow back)	characterised by appearance of hollow back in the lumbar region. The pelvis tends to be inclined forward, the abdominal muscles and hamstrings are lengthened and stretched, whereas the lumbar muscles are shortened and the gluteals weakened. the aim is to strengthen and shorten the abdominal muscles and hamstrings, strengthen the gluteal muscles and mobilise the lumbar spine. Lie on the floor with knees bent, feet slightly apart and hands resting on the thighs. Push down the small of the back into the floor until no gap exists. This will move the pelvis forward and tighten the abdominal muscles. Slowly lift the head and shoulders off the floor and return slowly to the starting position. Repeat over a period of time. *Remember to breathe in when raising the head and shoulders and breathe out when lowering back down.* NB: this condition is often accompanied by kyphosis.
kypho-lordosis	combination of kyphosis and lordosis. when corrective exercises are given, the lumbar spine must be corrected first, so the lordosis is not increased. When carrying out abdominal exercises, the thoracic region and the shoulders must be back and straight so as not to encourage the kyphosis.

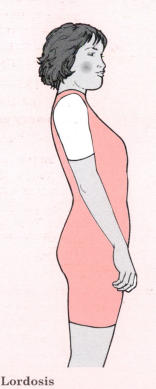

Lordosis

Table 3.10 (continued)

Condition	Exercise
scoliosis	characterised by a lateral curve of the spine going either to the right or the left side. The curvature tends to either be an 'S' or a 'C' shape. This type of fault causes changes in the muscles, ligaments, bones and joints which can lead to other faults such as one leg shorter than the other, one shoulder higher than the other, uneven scapula and pelvic tilt.

the aim with this condition is to restore the balance of the back muscles

- stride standing – carry out trunk side flexions sliding the hand down the concave side where two muscles are stretched
- prone lying – keeping the chin in, lift the head and shoulders, then lift the head and shoulders keeping hands clasped pulling down the arms

Scoliosis

| winged scapula | characterised by the inferior angle and the vertebral border of the scapula protruding backwards away from the ribs. This is apparent when the client lifts their arm forwards to shoulder level. The client will tend to have difficulty punching the arm forward, lifting the arm above shoulder level or performing any forward pushing movements. The problem tends to be in the serratus anterior |

the aim of these exercises is to strengthen the muscles which hold the scapula to the chest wall.

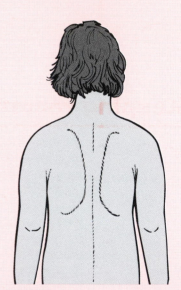

- stride standing, bending – punch a pillow/punch bag in a forward movement
- stride standing, arms bent – lean on a wall and push away from it
- prone lying – press up

Winged scapula

| weak abdominal muscles (visceroptosis) | abdominal and pelvic organs are displaced, usually downwards. It is usually caused by weak or overstretched abdominal muscles. Certain body types are prone to a weakness in the abdominal muscles, although certain factors such as pregnancy, operations, poor posture, lack of exercise, obesity and age can also cause weakened abdominal muscles. |

the therapist should be concerned with the strengthening of these muscles. However, finding out the cause of the weakness is of the utmost importance before commencing any form of treatment.

Table 3.10 *(continued)*

Condition	Exercise
dowagers hump	characterised by the head being tilted forward, this condition tends to affect females as they get older, although people can be born with the condition. If this is the case, the person is likely to be under medical supervision in which case you should not treat the client. If the condition has developed, it is probably as a result of fatty deposits accumulating at the back of the neck and over the spine which then become difficult to correct.

Dowagers hump

Keeping records

Once the consultation is complete, the therapist should ensure that all personal details and treatment recommendations are recorded and ask the client to sign the record card, once they have checked that all the details are correct.

Once a treatment has been carried out, you should record details of how the treatment went, contraindications, etc. Check that all mediums used are recorded on the form, and make a note of any modifications which were needed during the massage. You should also record any point which come out of the evaluation of the treatment and any comments which clients make about the effects of the treatment on subsequent visits.

Evaluating the treatment

Evaluating a treatment is an important part of client consultation. It is important that you evaluate every

CLIENT FEEDBACK

Client name:

Date of treatment:

Therapist's name:

Date:

	Yes *please comment*	**No** *please comment*
Were you made to feel welcome?	_____	_____
Did you discuss your treatment requirements before treatment?	_____	_____
Did you feel comfortable?	_____	_____
Were you happy with the therapist?	_____	_____
Were your needs met?	_____	_____
Did you feel relaxed during the treatment?	_____	_____
Were you happy with the home care advice?	_____	_____
Would you book another massage?	_____	_____

Thank you for your time, have you got any further comments that you would like to make?

_____

_____

_____

_____

Client's signature:

Date:

Evaluation form

treatment with feedback from clients wherever possible. This can be either formal or informal but whichever method you choose, ensure that it is simple for the client and provides you with all the information you need. You should analyse the results and take appropriate action, and remember to maintain client confidentiality at all times.

- oral questioning
  This can be as simple as asking the client if they have enjoyed and were satisfied with the treatment received.
- written feedback
  This can be achieved by asking the client to fill in a client treatment evaluation. An example is given below.

Dealing with client dissatisfaction

Remember that not all client feedback will be positive. However, unless the treatment was a complete disaster or the client is completely unreasonable, giving the client the opportunity to highlight areas where the treatment could be improved not only allows you to improve your treatment, but in most cases will make the client more likely to return. If the client is dealt with in an appropriate manner you can hopefully resolve the problem and retain the client. The following steps should be taken:

- take the client to a private area and listen to the complaint
- try to resolve it immediately
- record the complaint and action
- inform the insurers if necessary.

It is important to take client complaints seriously, as in some instances they may threaten legal action. Remember, never deal with any issues outside your responsibility.

Knowledge review – client consultation and contraindications to treatment

1   What is a contraindication?

2   When carrying out the client's consultation, you recognise treatment is contraindicated as the client has an infectious skin disorder. What action DO you take?

3   Name four infectious skin disorders.

4   Name three non-infectious skin conditions.

5   List the details you would include on a client's record card and explain why they are important.

6   Name eight contraindications to a body massage.

7   Describe the following conditions
   ● flat back
   ● kyphosis
   ● lordosis

8   What are the advantages of good posture?

9   How would you carry out an assessment of your client's posture?

10 List the three body types.

Preparation for massage

4

Learning objectives

This chapter covers the following:

- **preparation of the therapist**

- **preparation of the treatment area**

- **equipment**

- **preparation of the client**

This chapter covers the necessary preparation stages for massage of the therapist, the client and the treatment area. Before carrying out any massage treatment, it is important to prepare yourself, the treatment area and the client implementing all hygiene practices.

Preparation of the therapist

Appearance

The appearance of both yourself and your work environment is a reflection of your professionalism. Remember, first impressions count and your clients will judge you on the basis of these things. Clients will have confidence in you if you always look clean, well-groomed and smart.

Personal hygiene

As you are going to work in close proximity with your clients it is essential to clean yourself with daily bathing or showering. This will remove the sweat, dead cells and bacteria that cause body odour. An antiperspirant applied under the arms daily will help reduce perspiration, while a deodorant will mask the smell of sweat. Underwear should be clean and changed daily.

Oral hygiene

Teeth should be cleaned every morning, evening and after every meal. Dental floss should also be used. Breath fresheners and mouth washes may be required to freshen the breath. Remember to visit the dentist regularly to maintain healthy teeth.

Hands

It is essential that you wash your hands regularly, as they are covered in germs. Most of them are not harmful, but some can cause ill health and disease. It is essential to wash your hands after you have been to the toilet and before eating, as well as before and after treating each client, and if need be, during the treatment as well. This will minimise the risk of cross-infection and also convey an hygienic and professional image. When washing your hands, it is always more hygienic to use liquid soap (with a detergent containing chlorhexidine) from a sealed, disposable, dispenser. Disposable paper towels or warm air dryers should be used to dry the hands.

If you have any cuts or abrasions on your hands, it is important you cover them with a clean dressing to prevent the risk of secondary infection. Nail enamel should never be used when treating a client, as the client may be allergic. In

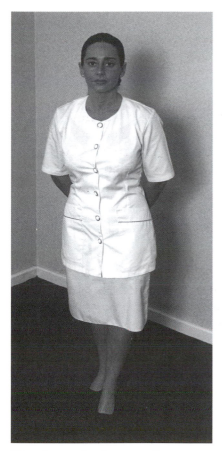

The therapist in overalls

Tip

Every salon/clinic has its own rules on dress, jewellery, etc. to reflect their own professional image. Find out what the dress code is in your place of work and adhere to it.

addition, nail enamel hides any dirt that is present underneath the nails so it is better to present visibly-clean, enamel-free nails to inspire confidence.

Feet

To ensure fresh and healthy feet, wash them daily, and you should always ensure they are dried thoroughly. Make sure your shoes are comfortable, fit properly and have a low comfortable heel. It is important to remember you are on your feet all day long. Foot sprays and medicated powders can be used to keep the feet dry and cool.

Hair

If hair is long it should be tied back securely to ensure it does not fall forwards, either over your own face or the face of the client when working. Hair should always be clean as well as tidy.

Clothing

You must wear a clean and pressed protective overall each day. Fabrics used for overalls are normally lightweight and comfortable to work in. Cotton is ideal as air can circulate, allowing perspiration to evaporate and therefore discourage body odour. The overall should be fairly loosely fitted and not too short. Most overalls are white as this signifies a clean image to clients. An overall may consist of a dress or tunic top with matching trousers.

Jewellery

Jewellery must be kept to a minimum. A flat wedding ring is acceptable but you should avoid wearing watchstraps or bracelets, which may catch the clients skin during treatment.

Posture

Posture is the way you hold yourself when walking, sitting and standing. Correct posture will enable you to work much longer without becoming tired, prevent stiff joints and muscle fatigue. It is important to stand:

- with the head up and balanced centrally
- shoulders should be relaxed but slightly back

- abdomen pulled in
- hips level
- bottom tucked in
- knees level
- weight evenly distributed and feet slightly apart.

Your posture should be very relaxed, as the arms need to be free and the hands in control. You should not work or stand with a hollow or bent back, rather the body weight should be supported by both feet and be upright. The strain imposed by heavier movements will be less fatiguing if the load is evenly distributed. Use the body weight to relieve any strain in the upper spine and the shoulder area. Once the client is positioned on the couch in a comfortable position, it is important that you can stand near to them, as having to reach will result in a poor massage for the client and strain on your arms and back.

Stance

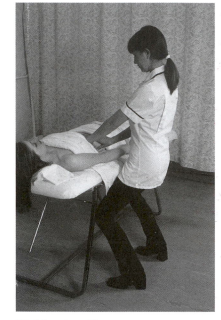

Stride standing

How you stand when performing the massage is of great importance. Two standing positions are commonly used. These are:

1 **Stride standing** In this position, the feet are placed two foot lengths apart and the weight is distributed between them.
2 **Walk standing** In this position, one foot is placed in front of the other, two lengths between the heels, and weight is evenly distributed.

You can pivot freely from walk standing to stride standing and vice versa, during the massage. When working longitudinally along the length of the muscle fibres, you stand in walk standing and when massaging transversely across the muscle fibres, you can swivel into stride standing.

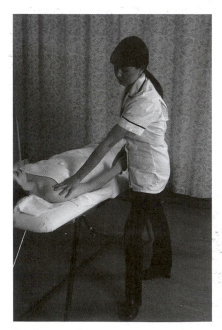

Walk standing

Poor technique results when the feet are in the wrong position because the body weight is thrown out of balance, which affects the rhythm, depth and smoothness. As well as resulting in a poor massage, this can also lead to a bad back. Although you will tend to sway slightly backwards and forwards when completing sweeping movements, to help body rhythm, unnecessary movements should be avoided as they are a waste of energy and can distract the client. Body weight can be used to regulate the pressure and massage movements as they are applied.

Tip

Remember, the nails should always be well-manicured with the nail plate short and unvarnished.

Hand exercises

Your hands should be soft and smooth, with both the hands and joints supple and relaxed. In order to achieve this suppleness, you will have to practise the following exercises, in order that both hands work equally as well, and your joints become mobile and flexible.

1 Make a tight fist, hold it for a few seconds and then quickly unclench, stretching out your fingers as far as possible.

2 Roll the wrists round and round going one way and then the other.

3 Rotate the hands from the wrist, first one way and then the other.

4 Place the index fingers and thumbs together and stretch them as far out as possible.

5 Place hands in a praying position, keeping the fingers together, try and lift out the palms.

6 Still in the praying position press the fingers against each other one by one, keeping the palms together.

7 Wave the wrist from side to side and then up and down.

8 Place alternate fingers down on hard surface as if playing a piano.

9 Rotate fists in a circular motion.

10 Knead a soft ball.

Hand exercises, step 2

Hand exercises, step 5

Hand exercises, step 6

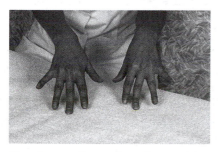

Hand exercises, step 8

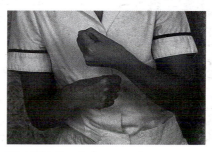

Hand exercises, step 9

Mental preparation

Before starting the massage, you must try and feel calm and relaxed and shut out anything that may distract you and focus only on the client. When dealing with several clients you need to 'switch off' in-between each one. If you can do this, you will not feel as tired at the end of the day.

It is important not to let the client drain you, by not taking on board their problems, just listen and then forget once they leave. Otherwise, you will become too involved emotionally and this will leave you physically drained.

Preparation of the treatment area

Hygiene

Hygiene is very important as it prevents cross-infection and secondary infection. These occur through poor practice such as failing to recognise skin diseases or failing to carry out the correct hygiene procedures. **Cross-infection** occurs when contagious micro-organisms are transferred because sterilisation procedures are not being adhered to. **Secondary infections** can occur as a result of injury to the client during treatment, or if the client already has an open wound and bacteria penetrates the skin and causes an infection.

Tip

Remember – Never eat or drink in the treatment area.

General rules regarding hygiene

- Wherever possible use disposable products.
- All work surfaces, including trolleys and massage beds, must be wiped with a chlorine preparation, always follow the manufacturer's instructions. These must be clean and covered with disposable paper tissue.
- Each client should have clean towels and gowns. All dirty laundry must be placed in a covered container.
- All waste must be placed in a suitable container lined with a disposable bag.

Sterilisation and sanitisation can minimise or destroy harmful micro-organisms which could cause an infection. Sterilisation is a complete destruction of all living organisms and sanitisation is the destruction of some but not all the micro-organisms. These techniques are practised in salons and clinics and involve the use of chemical agents – antiseptic, disinfectants, vapour fumigants and physical agents such as heat and radiation.

Radiation (sterilisation)

Ultraviolet (UV) light from a quartz mercury lamp can be used to destroy micro-organisms, although this has limited uses and cannot be totally effective.

The UV bulb is contained in a closed cabinet that can be used to store objects that have been sterilised.

UV cabinet

Heat (sterilisation)

Dry and moist heat can be used to sterilise implements. The most effective method of heat sterilisation is the use of the **autoclave** which is very similar to a pressure cooker. The temperature reaches 121–134°C when increased pressure is created.

Another method is a **glass bead steriliser**. This is a small unit containing glass beads which are electrically heated. The glass beads transfer heat to the objects they come into contact with and sterilise them.

Disinfectants and antiseptics (sanitisation)

If for some reason an object cannot be sterilised, it must be wiped with surgical spirit and placed in a chemical disinfectant solution like glutaraldehyde or a quaternary ammonium compound. A disinfectant will not, however, destroy all micro-organisms. After the implements are removed from the disinfectant, they must be rinsed in clean water to remove all traces of the solution and in order to prevent an allergic reaction on the client's skin.

An antiseptic is much milder than a disinfectant and can, therefore, be applied to the skin, but it does have limited effect. Like disinfectants, antiseptics will not kill all the micro-organisms.

Remember from the previous section that infectious diseases that are contagious contraindicate body treatments, and in some cases, clients with non-contagious skin disorders should not receive massage treatment as it could result in a secondary infection. When practising massage, strict hygiene is required in order to prevent the risk of exposure and cross infection.

Equipment

Everything must be prepared before the client arrives for the massage treatment. You must make sure that you have everything to hand.

Treatment room checklist

✓ client record card
✓ massage couch prepared with clean linen and blankets
✓ spare pillows and towels
✓ clean gown for the client
✓ screens to ensure privacy
✓ comfortable room temperature
✓ soft lighting
✓ minimal noise level
✓ trolley laid out with:
   ✓ massage mediums
   ✓ tissues
   ✓ bowls
   ✓ cotton wool
   ✓ antiseptic solution
   ✓ any other materials that may be used in the treatment

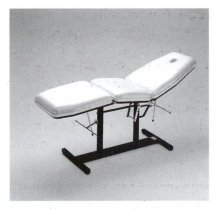

Massage couch

Stool

Screen

Equipment trolley

It is really important to make sure that you have everything that you might need, as it disrupts the treatment and gives a poor impression, if you have to break away because you have forgotten something. It is also extremely important that the trolley is always within reach so that you can turn and reach anything on the trolley but leave your other hand in contact with the client.

Lubricants

Part of the preparation of a treatment room is preparing the massage medium. The choice of massage medium is very important, in order to provide an effective treatment. Sometimes the client may state which medium they prefer, but usually you choose it to compliment the skin type. When clients do request a certain cream or oil, this is sometimes because they believe in what the manufacturer claims their preparations can do, and the client feels it will give added value to their treatment.

Remember always apply the lubricant to your hands first, warm it in your palms and then apply it to the client. If at the end of the massage, there is an excessive amount of lubricant left on the client, you can wipe it off with an eau de cologne, or a warm damp towel, according to the client's preference.

All massage lubricants should be used sparingly, and always applied on your hands first and never directly onto the client. There are different types of emollients to choose from.

Powder

Always keep the use of powder to a minimum. If an excessive amount is used, the pores will become clogged. You should always powder your hands rather than the client's body, as powder is of no benefit to the client. Its function is to provide slip for your hands if they are a little sticky. You should only ever use the finest of powders, unscented and unperfumed if possible, to avoid irritation of the skin. Powder is particularly good for oily skin. Remember, if the skin is dry, powder irritates the condition and can sometime make normal skin feel dry.

Oil

Oil is used in a massage to produce a much deeper effect than powder. It enables the therapist to stretch the tissues and increase the depth of the massage, as it enables the hands to glide easily without rubbing or tearing the skin. Oil tends to nourish and soften the skin, and it is particularly good for dry skin conditions. If too much oil is used, the tissues will slide away from your hands, producing too much slip and a very superficial massage. The only disadvantage with oil is that it can leave the client with a greasy feeling after the treatment.

Cream

Creams are absorbed more readily into the skin and are excellent for use on very hairy areas. Clients will often choose a cream, as they feel they have a special quality that enhances and softens the skin. The disadvantage with using a cream is that the hands begin to drag and you will need to keep stopping to reapply it. It is particularly good for dry to normal skin type.

Essential oils

Essential oils can also be used as a massage medium. They should always be mixed with a carrier oil and **never**

Tip

Sometimes the client may be unclean, particularly their feet. Therefore, it may be appropriate to wash the client discreetly before massaging that area and incorporate it into the treatment, so the client will not be offended.

applied undiluted. Most essential oils have therapeutic and curative effects on the body's systems and blends can be made to the specific client's requirements. Essential oils must only be used by a qualified aromatherapist and some are contraindicated for certain conditions. See Chapter 9.

Preparation of the client

Always greet the client warmly and take them personally along to the treatment room. If it is the client's first treatment, it is essential they are put at ease. It is at this stage that you should carry out the consultation (covered in the previous chapter), making sure you obtain and record all the necessary information. It is important on the first visit to check that that they have no medical conditions which would contraindicate the treatment. In the consultation, you should explain the treatment to the client and make sure that they have an opportunity to ask any questions.

Once the client is ready, you should ask them to change into a gown and unless a pre-heat treatment is to be carried out first, assist them onto the massage couch. The client should always have use of a foot stool in order to get up onto the massage couch. If you feel they need further assistance, it is important to support the client onto the couch.

The client should be settled comfortably and in a position where there will be a minimum amount of disturbance for the full treatment. The position will vary depending on whether the treatment is localised or a full body massage. (See Chapter 6). The client must be supported throughout the treatment by pillows, and it is important to ensure that only the areas being massaged are exposed. The rest of the body should be covered by clean blankets or towels to ensure warmth and modesty are preserved.

Knowledge review – preparation for massage

1 State four basic requirements for maintaining personal hygiene.

2 Why is it important that you wash your hands before carrying out a massage treatment?

3 Define the terms:
- sterilisation
- cross-infection
- secondary infection

4 Name the different types of lubricants and state one disadvantage for each.

5 Describe the two different standing positions that should be adopted when massaging a client.

6 What is the purpose of carrying out hand exercises prior to carrying out a massage?

7 List the items that should be prepared before the client arrives for treatment.

8 State how you would prepare your client for the treatment.

Pre-heat treatments

Learning objectives

This chapter covers the following:

- **purpose of pre-heat treatments**
- **types of pre-heat treatments**

This chapter covers the main types of heat treatments that can be applied to a client before their massage is given. The pre-heat treatments covered in this chapter are paraffin wax, infrared, steam, sauna, spa, foam and hydro.

Purpose of pre-heat treatments

Pre-heat treatments are often applied prior to massage in order to:

- relax the client and warm the body
- soothe any pain the client may suffer
- alleviate any tension.

Heat can be applied to the whole body or to isolated areas such as joints. You will have to ascertain during the consultation whether or not a pre-heat treatment would be useful/necessary. NB: Case Study 2 in the back of the book describes a situation where pre-heat treatment was used.

There are a number of pre-heat methods and the main ones are examined in turn in the following sections.

Types of pre-heat treatments

Paraffin wax

The benefits of paraffin wax:

- warms the muscles
- promotes relaxation
- softens the skin and aids desquamation, therefore improving the skin texture
- increases the circulation
- improves conditions such as arthritic joints and any stiffness, helping to increase mobility
- relieves pain.

Contraindications

- skin diseases and disorders
- undiagnosed lumps and bumps
- severe bruising or swellings.

Procedure

Paraffin wax is suitable as a pre-heat treatment for either part or all of the body. Once a consultation has taken place and you have ensured that there are no contraindications:

1 Apply a thin coat of nourishing cream to the area.

2 Heated the wax to approximately 37°C and transfer it to a bowl.

3 Test the temperature of the wax by applying a small amount to the back of your wrist.

4 Apply wax to the body with a brush. You should apply about five layers, allowing the previous layer to dry before applying the next.

5 Cover the waxed area with tin foil and towels to retain the heat and leave to cool.

6 Once the wax has cooled, remove by peeling. The treated area will be warm, relaxed and ready for the massage.

Infrared treatment

Infrared radiation has longer wavelengths than daylight or light from light bulbs, thus its red colour. It can be felt as warmth on the area of the body that is being treated.

The infrared rays penetrate into the epidermis, producing heat which warms and soothes the skin. It can:

- increase circulation
- increase lymphatic flow
- relax muscles in preparation for massage
- relieve muscular and joint pain.

Contraindications

- skin disorders
- diabetes (because circulation is poor as is skin sensation)
- loss of skin sensation
- sunburn
- metal plates or pins
- circulatory or heart problems.

Procedure

You should always follow the manufacturer's instructions and check for contraindications prior to treatment.

1 A skin test must be carried out prior to the treatment to test the client's sensitivity. Fill two test tubes – one with warm water and the other with cold. Ask the client to

close their eyes and test the tubes on the areas that are to be exposed to the heat. If the client can distinguish between hot and cold, their sensitivity is normal and the treatment may continue. If they cannot tell the difference, you should not use pre-heat treatment.

2   Ensure that all grease is removed from the client's skin. You can either invite them to take a shower or wipe the skin with a tonic.

3   Position the client covering the areas you do not want to expose to the lamp. Do not forget to protect the client's eyes. The lamp should be warmed-up prior to starting the treatment.

4   Position the lamp at the right angle to achieve maximum intensity. Never have the lamp directly over the client. Position the lamp at the correct distance from the client between 40 to 55cm depending on the generator output. If you increase the distance of the lamp from the client, the client will receive the same amount of radiation but it will be more gentle and slow. If the distance from the lamp to the client is doubled, the client will require four times the original amount of time to produce the same effect. If the distance is halved, the intensity becomes four times greater.

5   The infrared treatment can last from 10 to 20 minutes.

6   At the end of the treatment, position the lamp well away from the client for safety reasons.

Technical note

Distance and timing are based on the principles of the inverse square law. The inverse square law says that the closer the lamp is to the body, the higher the heat intensity will be and conversely, the further away the lamp is placed, the less intense, as the rays spread over a much larger area.

Wet and dry heat treatments

Steam and sauna are the two main types of wet and dry heat treatments respectively. The following benefits and contraindications apply to both:

- circulation increases
- lactic acid disperses from the muscles via increased circulation
- skin colour improves as an erythema is produced
- sweat glands are stimulated which helps to eliminate waste products
- heart beat quickens and body temperature rises
- muscles relax.

Contraindications

- prescribed medication (obtain medical permission)
- skin diseases

- epilepsy
- diabetes
- high or low blood pressure
- thrombosis
- coronary thrombosis
- lung conditions, asthma, bronchitis, hay fever
- pregnancy (later stages)
- heavy menstruation
- heavy meal or excess alcohol consumed just prior to treatment.

Types of heat therapy

Steam bath

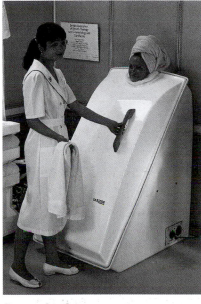

Steam bath

Steam baths produce a moist heat as water is heated to produce the steam. The cabinet has a door and an opening at the top for the head. There is a seat with a tank underneath it, in which the water is heated. Steam baths can be made from metal or fibreglass. Metal steam baths have a tendency to get very hot and to compensate for this, the client must be protected by towels. This is not necessary with fibreglass steam baths.

Procedure

The steam bath should be cleaned and you should check that there is enough water in the tank prior to the client arriving. You should prepare the seat with towels and switch the bath on approximately 15 minutes before the client arrives. The temperature needs to be between 50–55°C.

When the client arrives, you should carry out a consultation, and if everything is okay for the treatment to proceed, you should ask the client to have a shower. Once the bath has reached the correct temperature, you should help the client into the bath, tucking a towel firmly around the neck to prevent steam from escaping. You should demonstrate how the client can leave the cabinet if they wish to do so before their treatment time has finished. (They may begin to feel claustrophobic). Treatment time is between 10 and 20 minutes depending on the individual, but this maximum should never be exceeded. After the treatment has finished, the client should have a warm shower prior to their massage. The cabinet must be cleaned thoroughly with a disinfectant solution.

Sauna bath

Sauna baths

The sauna is another form of heat treatment. It has similar effects to the steam bath but uses dry rather than moist heat. Saunas are usually made from panels of log with insulating material between them to prevent heat from escaping. The floor is also pine so it does not become too hot to stand on. Pine is ideal as it keeps dry and absorbs condensation, as well as absorbing the heat and radiating it back into the sauna.

Inside the sauna are resting benches, duckboards, a bucket and ladle, an electric stove and a rail for the stove. The heat is produced from the electric stove which is controlled by a thermostat positioned as near to the ceiling as possible in order to give an accurate reading.

Benefits

These are largely the same as the steam baths, although there is more sweating. This evaporates quickly leaving the skin dry.

Procedure

The sauna must be switched on at least 30 minutes prior to treatment. The temperature is normally set at 70°C. Towels should be placed on the benches and the bucket filled with water.

Prior to treatment you should carry out a full consultation, during which you should explain the treatment fully to the client. It is beneficial to advise the client to start on a lower bench before moving up to a higher one where it is hotter. Treatment time is usually from 15 to 20 minutes, and water should be poured onto the coals occasionally, as this will produce more heat. You should let the client know that they can take cool showers at intervals throughout the treatment.

The sauna should be cleaned on a regular basis with disinfectant, and at the end of the day it is advisable to leave the sauna door open to eliminate any smells.

Other pre-heat treatments

Other pre-heat treatments include spa baths, foam baths and hydro-oxygen baths.

- **spa baths** are large baths that can accommodate a number of people at the same time. A gentle overall massage is produced by bubbles that come through air channels underneath and from the sides of the bath.

Spa bath

- **foam baths** are more frequently found on health farms. They are similar to ordinary baths but produce foam heated to about 40°C. The client semi-reclines in the bath, with only the head visible. This treatment relaxes the muscles and induces perspiring.
- **hydro-oxygen baths** are cabinets in which the client reclines while hot water jets squirt the body. It is important to check the client for contraindications prior to the treatment and never leave them unsupervised.

Knowledge review – pre-heat treatments

1 Describe the different pre-heat treatments available to a client.

2 What are the benefits of each treatment?

3 Give the main contraindications for:
- paraffin wax
- infrared
- wet and dry heat treatments

Massage techniques and procedures

6

Learning objectives

This chapter covers the following:

- **massage movements**
- **massage routines and duration**
- **aftercare**

This chapter describes basic massage techniques and procedures, including the commercially accepted timings for treatments.

Massage movements

There are five classifications of massage movements. These are:

1   effleurage including stroking movements
2   petrissage, or compressions
3   tapotement, or percussions.
4   frictions
5   vibrations.

Effleurage (stroking)

Effleurage is a sweeping, stroking movement. Its main uses are at the beginning and the end of the massage sequence and as a connecting or link movement that can be used at any point during the massage procedure. Effleurage introduces the client to massage. It allows them to get used to the therapist's touch, to become sensitised to the underlying muscles and tissues while at the same time enabling a massage medium to be applied to the area. This movement has a soothing and relaxing effect.

Effleurage is performed with the palm of the hand or pads of the fingers, depending on the size of the area to be massaged and the amount of pressure to be applied. Effleurage movements can be either superficial or deep. Effleurage should be performed with relaxed hands moulding to the body's contours. The fingers should be relaxed and held closely together and the thumbs should also be relaxed and abducted. Effleurage movements follow the direction of the venous blood return to the heart, applying more pressure on the upward movement than on the return.

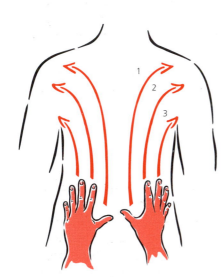

Effleurage

Health & Safety

Any medical oedema, i.e. any oedema with a systemic cause, for example, kidney malfunction, is contraindicated for massage.

Benefits

The benefits of the effleurage movement are:

- soothing effect on the nerves, inducing relaxation
- increases both blood and lymphatic circulation
- aids relief of tension, by relaxing contracted, tense muscles
- aids desquamation, the removal of dead cells

● helps to reduce non-medical oedema, which is a result of poor circulation and tiredness.

Petrissage

These strokes are deeper than those of effleurage and usually applied with the thumbs, fingers or heels of hands. These movements are characterised by firmly picking up and lifting the tissues from the underlying structures and then releasing, resulting in an intermittent pressure. All these movements relieve muscular tension, fatigue and stiffness. Petrissage manipulations include kneading, picking up, wringing, and rolling.

Kneading

Kneading movements may be performed in several ways. The technique can be achieved using both hands, one hand or just part of the hand – palmar, double-handed or single-handed kneading. Pressure is applied firmly then released. The movement is then repeated in an adjacent area. The pressure must always be applied towards the heart. Care must be taken to avoid pinching the skin at the end of the strokes.

Picking up

This movement can be performed with one or both hands, depending on the area to be massaged. For example, if movement is to be carried out on the deltoid muscle, then one hand is used and the muscle can be massaged either side. The technique is to grasp the muscle with the whole hand with the thumb abducted. The muscle is lifted away from the underlying structure, squeezed and then released

Technical tip

Reinforced movements
Any technique where one hand [ironing], or fingers, are placed over the corresponding hand or fingers will give a deeper pressure. This is known as a reinforced movement.

Palmer kneading　　　Double-handed kneading　　　Single-handed kneading

again. On relaxation the other hand picks up a different part and the movement is repeated along the length of the muscle. It is important to ensure that contact is not broken between movements.

Wringing

The muscle is lifted from the underlying structures and then moved from side to side across the muscle length with the fingers of one hand working with the thumb of the opposite hand. The tissue is grasped and stretched.

Rolling

Hands are placed firmly on the area. The superficial tissues are grasped between the fingers and thumbs and gently rolled backwards and forwards against the thumbs and fingers.

Benefits of petrissage

- increases blood and lymph circulation bringing fresh nutrients to the organs and speeding up the removal of waste products
- increases venous return
- breaks down tension nodules in the muscles and therefore helps to prevent the formation of fibrosis in the muscle. This is especially the case for the trapezius muscle of the upper back
- speeds up the removal of waste products built up in the tissues aiding the absorption of fluid, particularly around the joints
- aids relaxation.

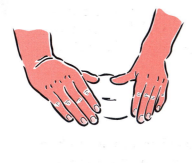

Picking up

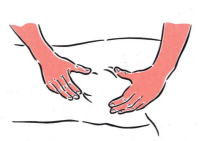

Wringing

Rolling

Tapotement (Percussion)

These movements are used for stimulating and toning the area where they are used. Tapotement movements include cupping (clapping), hacking, beating and pounding. The client must have sufficient muscle bulk or mass to perform this movement, otherwise it could be very painful and lead to bruising. Consequently, these movements should not be used on the thin or elderly. These types of movements should be light and springy and should not cause any discomfort to the client. Wrists need to be loose and flexible. Tapotement movements increase the circulation, which can create a healthy glow, thereby improving appearance.

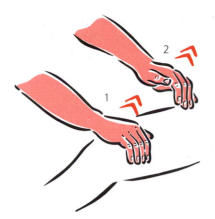

Cupping

Cupping

Cupping is performed with the hands forming loose cups, which then strike the area being massaged making a very distinctive clapping sound. An **erythema** (reddening) is produced quickly due to the vacuum that is formed in the **palmar** surfaces as they contact the tissues.

Hacking

Hacking

Hacking is a very fast and light movement. The hands face each other but do not touch and the hands tend to be at right angles to the wrists. The fingers flick against the skin very quickly in rapid succession. The outer three fingers tend to do all the striking. Hacking is a very stimulating movement, stimulating both the circulation and the sensory nerve endings.

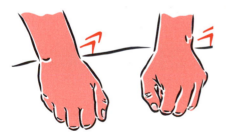

Beating

Beating

Beating can be performed slowly or quickly, depending on the type of effect you want to achieve. The hands form a loose fist with the arms relaxed and from shoulder level they strike the client's body. The colour of the skin changes, producing an erythema as the temperature of the skin rises.

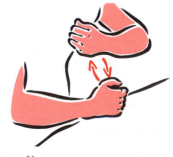

Pounding

Pounding

Pounding is performed with the outer borders of the hands, with the hands held loosely but closed. The movement comes from the therapist's elbows and forearms. This movement is very rapid and is as stimulating as the beating movements.

Tip

Tapotement movements should not be performed directly over the spine. Always ensure the hands are loose and relaxed to avoid any discomfort to the client or bruising occurring.

The tapotement movements increase the circulation, improve muscle tone and stimulate sensory nerve endings.

Benefits of tapotement

- aids sluggish circulation
- helps loosen mucus in chest conditions, when performed over the thoracic region
- tones and strengthen muscles
- produces local erythema due to a localised rise in the skin temperature
- stimulates sensory nerve endings, therefore bringing about vasodilation of blood vessels.

Tapotement movements are particularly good for cellulite conditions, as they stimulate the skin's surface and the underlying tissues, which then improves their appearance, often likened to orange peel. Cellulite conditions can affect any type of client regardless of their age, body shape or weight. Cellulite usually occurs around the tensor fascia latea muscle (lateral aspect of the thigh), the rectus abdominus muscle (abdomen), the gluteals (buttocks) and the tricep muscles (back of the arm).

Thumb and finger frictions

Frictions

Frictions are usually applied in small areas of the surface tissue. They are rubbing movements where the skin is rubbed against deeper underlying structures. The movements are applied with a circular technique using the tips of the thumbs and fingers, and applying a degree of stretch to the underlying structures. These types of movements help to break down fibrous thickenings, fatty deposits and aid the removal of any non-medical oedema.

Tip

A quick test to carry out to see if oedema is medical or non-medical is to gently press the centre of the swelling. If the indentation made in the skin springs back, then this is a non-medical oedema. If it takes a few minutes to return to normal, it is a medical oedema, and a doctor's advice must be sought by the client.

Benefits of frictions

- helps to break down tight nodules
- aids in relaxation
- increases lymph and blood circulation.

Vibrations

These movements are used to relieve fatigue. They also relieve pain by stimulating the nerves, which produces a sedative effect on the area. Vibrations are fine trembling

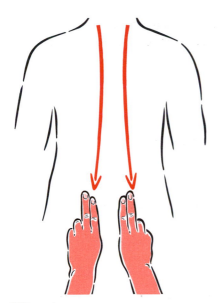

Vibrations

movements which can be performed with either one or both hands. Vibration movements can be **static**, that is performed in one place, or **running**, that is moving up or down. Using the palmar surface of the hand, the pads of the fingers or the distal phalanx of the thumbs (this is the smallest bone in the thumb and forms the tip of the thumb), the muscles of the forearm are contracted continually and then relaxed to produce the vibration movements.

Benefits of vibrations

- clear and stimulate the nerve pathways
- relieve tension in the neck and back, inducing relaxation
- can help increase the action of the lungs
- helps to increase peristalsis in the colon.

Massage routines and duration

Tip

A massage treatment should include a full range of movements, chosen to suit the client. If the client is especially tense in the upper neck and shoulder region, the therapist should adapt the manipulations and spend more time concentrating on this area and less time on other areas of the body.

The commercially acceptable timing for a full Swedish body massage is approximately 60 minutes. The only areas that are not usually massaged are the face and scalp. The time spent on individual body parts, unless it is decided otherwise during the consultation, is as follows:

- neck and chest – 5 minutes
- arms – 5 minutes each
- abdomen – 5 minutes
- legs – 10 minutes each
- buttocks – 5 minutes (optional)
- back – 15 minutes.

Often a client will book for just a partial massage, so you can use the timings above as a guide.

Once the technique has been grasped, the basic procedures outlined below can be adapted to suit anyone's needs. You should have established your client's requirements in the consultation and adapted the massage appropriately. The massage technique should always be performed throughout by moulding your hands to the contours of the clients body, smoothly and rhythmically. No break in the continuity should ever occur; contact with the client must be maintained at all times.

The massage technique should generally be deep (unless there is any reason why this is contraindicated), using your body weight in the movements on the back and lower limbs is essential. The rate of the massage should be moderate, unless the client requests it to be slower or faster.

For a full body massage, the client will usually lie in the supine (face upwards) position at the start of the massage to have the front of their body massaged first, turning over to the prone position later, so the massage concludes with their back. The client should be in a position which requires minimal movement throughout the treatment, but when the client needs to move or turn over, you must support the client's body to help them. The reason for working in this order is that in most cases massaging the back will be the most relaxing. Finishing on this area maximises the effect of the massage, as the client should become progressively more relaxed. In addition, if clients want to talk to you, they will usually do this at the beginning of the massage, and this is easier if they are supine.

Procedure

- Assist the client to lie on the couch in a supine position, using pillows to support the head, back of neck and under the knee. Massage the body parts in the following order:

  1 right arm
  2 left arm
  3 neck and chest
  4 abdomen
  5 right leg
  6 left leg

- Turn the client over into the prone position (face down), again using pillows to support the face, neck and shoulders, under the front of the abdomen and hips, and under the front of the ankles. Massage the body parts in the following order:

  7 gluteals and buttocks
  8 back

The massage technique is always adapted to suit the clients needs. For example, if the client does not wish their gluteals to be included in the massage and complains of tension in the upper shoulders, more time could be spent on that area. You will have found this out during your pre-treatment consultation.

If the client is male, the massage is usually performed with greater depth using all of your body weight. See Chapter 7 for the adaptations that you might need.

Tip

When only one hand is massaging, the other should be supporting the limb that is being worked on.

Arm massage

The client can either be lying on their back or with their head and back supported with pillows. The client's arm should be supported by a pillow. You should be in the walk standing position outlined on page 130.

1   Effluerage to cover the whole arm from finger tips up towards the axilla glands. Supporting the client's arm, your left hand works on the back of the arm and the right hand on the front of the arm. Each hand works alternately until the client is relaxed. (9 times)

2   Continue to support the client's arm and apply deep effleurage to the deltoid muscle, contouring the hand around the muscle. Rotate the movement clockwise and repeat anticlockwise. (3 times)

3   Perform single-handed kneading, alternating, to the bicep and tricep muscles, working upwards with the movement and then sliding back down to the elbow. (3 times)

4   Stand in the stride position and perform picking up to the deltoid muscle. (3 times)

5   Apply picking up to the tricep and bicep muscles. (3 times)

6   Apply wringing to deltoid, tricep and bicep muscles. (3 times)

7   Apply finger kneading to the elbow. Back to walk standing. (3 times)

8   Kneading to forearm and hand. (3 times)

9   Picking up to forearm. Pick up the extensors and flexors working from the elbow to the wrist and slide back up to the elbow. In stride standing. (3 times)

10 Thumb kneading to interosseous membrane (the gap between the radius and ulna bones), working up to the elbow with small controlled movements and then sliding back down to the wrist. In walk standing. (3 times)

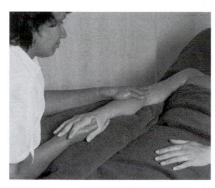

Arm massage step 1

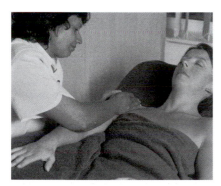

Arm massage step 2

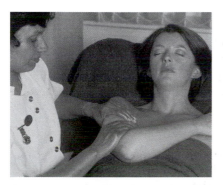

Arm massage step 4

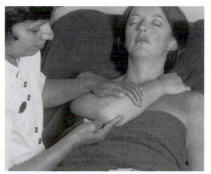

Arm massage step 7

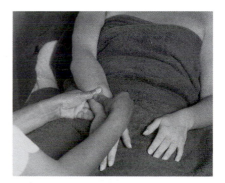

Arm massage step 10

Tip

Remember not to touch the breast tissue when massaging this area.

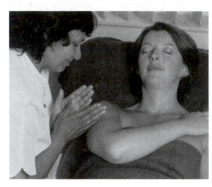

Arm massage step 12

11   Thumb kneading to the wrist and tendons of the hand joint, fingers and palm of hand, adapting the pressure so as not to cause discomfort. (3 times)

12   If the client has sufficient tissue present, perform hacking to the whole arm in the stride standing position. Support the client's arm placing the hand of the opposite shoulder on the lateral aspect of the upper arm and perform hacking up and down the arm from the shoulder to elbow. (3 times)

13   Change to walk standing position and complete work on this area by performing effluerage as before. (9 times)

14   Place the client's arm back on the couch and cover with the blanket before repeating the procedure with the other arm.

Neck and chest massage

The client can be either lying on their back or sitting, with pillows placed behind the head to ensure the neck and chest muscles are relaxed. Start the routine in walk standing position.

1   Facing the client effleurage across the clavicle, around the shoulders and up behind the neck, adapting the pressure to suit the client. Your hands should keep in contact with the client. As your hands slide back to the sternum, cross them over and effleurage to the deltoids. Keeping the hands on the deltoid, hold for a few seconds, and apply a slight stretch to the area. (6 times)

2   In the stride standing position, apply alternate stroking to the chest from axilla to axilla, ensuring one hand starts as the other is leaving the body. (6 times)

3   Perform double handed kneading over the chest, adapting the pressure to suit the client. (3 times)

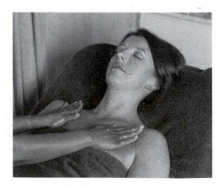   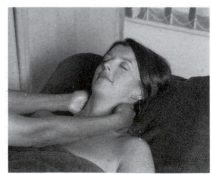   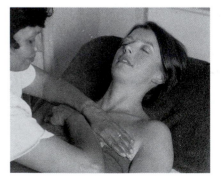

Neck and chest step 1

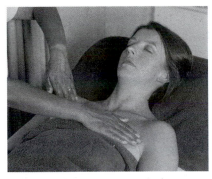

Neck and chest step 2

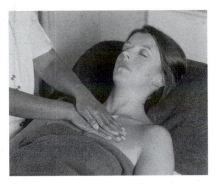

Neck and chest step 3

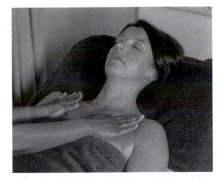

4 Keeping the hands in contact with the client, walk round to the top of the couch and thumb knead the trapezius muscle working inwards from the shoulders up the occiput and sliding back round. (6 times)

5 Go back to walk standing and facing the client finger knead the clavicle using the index and middle finger. (3 times)

6 In the stride standing position, apply light hacking over the pectoral muscles, if appropriate.

7 In the walk standing position, conclude the neck and chest massage with effleurage. (6 times)

Abdominal massage

The client should be lying on their back, with their knees flexed and well supported.

1 In the walk standing position, carry out diamond effleurage by placing the hands on the waist. Effleurage up to the sternum, back to the waist and then down to the pubic symphysis. (3 times)

2 Apply alternate kneading to the lateral walls of the abdomen. (3 times)

Tip

1 It is more comfortable for the client if the bladder is empty.

2 Never massage on a full stomach.

3 Maintain the client's modesty by placing a towel over the chest area and pulling it down to the hips.

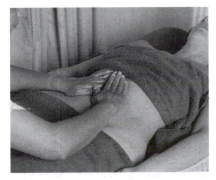

Abdominal massage step 1

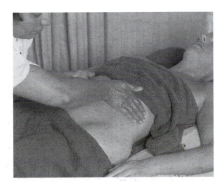

Abdominal massage step 2

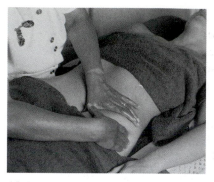

Abdominal massage step 3

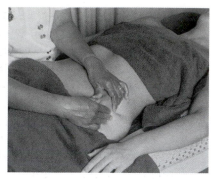

Abdominal massage step 4

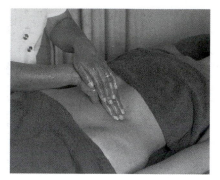

Abdominal massage step 5

3   In the stride standing position, apply wringing to the lateral walls if the client has sufficient subcutaneous tissue. If there is insufficient tissue, wringing will be uncomfortable for the client. (3 times)

4   Apply skin rolling to the lateral walls. Place the palms of the hands underneath the posterior aspect of the abdomen and the thumbs on the anterior aspect. Roll the thumbs down towards the palms of the hands with visible skin underneath the thumbs.

5   In the walk standing position, apply finger kneading to the colon starting from the right-hand side of the client's pelvis. Work up over the ascending colon to waist level. Swing into the stride standing position and continue to knead across the transverse colon. At the left side, swing back into walk standing position and continue to knead down over the descending colon, towards the left groin. This to stimulate peristalsis and aids constipation.

   If the client prefers, this movement can be carried out with a stroking movement with one hand starting as the other one is leaving the body.

6   In the walk standing position, conclude the abdominal massage with effleurage.

Leg massage

The client is massaged either in a lying position or in the 'long' sitting position. The leg being treated should rest on a pillow in a relaxed outward rotation, knee and hip flexed slightly and the ankle and foot free. Ensure the client's modesty is maintained by placing a towel in the middle of the legs and only having the leg which is to be worked on uncovered. Full support is required for the heavy lower limbs, which means frequent changing of pillow positions, this should on no account affect the rhythm and continuity of the massage procedure.

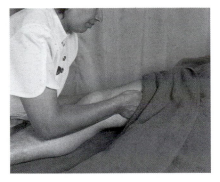

Leg massage step 1

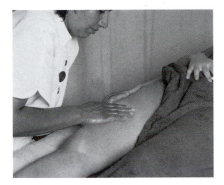

Leg massage step 2

1   Standing in the walk standing position at the client's ankle, effleurage the whole leg from the toes up to the femoral triangle, covering the anterior, medial and lateral walls. Apply pressure upwards, and ease pressure when returning to the tarsals. (3 times)

2   Starting at the lateral aspect of the thigh, with one hand apply hand kneading from the hip to the patella. Place the other hand on the medial aspect of the thigh below the femoral triangle and when both hands are parallel, knead together down to the patella. This movement can be repeated using alternate kneading movements. (3 times)

3   Slide the palms around the anterior and posterior aspect of the legs so they are placed on the hamstrings and quadriceps, and alternately knead the muscles. If the client is large, placing a bolster underneath the patella will make this movement easier. (3 times)

4   In the stride standing position, carry out hacking and clapping movements from the patella to the groin area and back down. This is particularly good to stimulate circulation and therefore aids conditions such as cellulite and poor circulation.

5   In the walk standing position, perform effleurage to the upper thigh. (3 times)

6   Perform finger kneading around the patella in slow rhythmical movements. (3 times)

7   In the walk standing position, flex and support the client's knee with one hand and with the other knead up and down the gastrocnemus and the lateral side of the lower leg. (3 times)

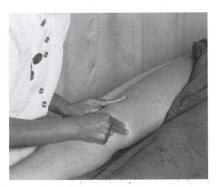

Leg massage step 6

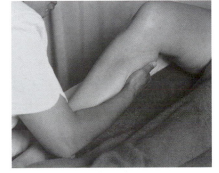

Leg massage step 7

8   Stand at the bottom of the couch in the walk standing position and working upwards, thumb knead the tibialis anterior on the outer shin. (3 times)

9   Working on the feet, place hands on either side of the toes and press gently together. Rotate all the toes clockwise and anticlockwise. (3 times)

10   Effleurage the foot. (3 times)

11   In the walk standing position at the client's ankle, conclude the leg massage by applying effleurage to the whole leg. (3 times)

Gluteals and buttocks massage

The gluteals are worked on one side at a time, keeping a towel over the area not being massaged to avoid over exposure of the area. Stand on the opposite side to the gluteal being massaged which enables you to work inwards with the massage movements.

1   In the walk standing position, support the nearside gluteal with one hand and apply effleurage to the farside gluteal with the other hand. Work inwards to cover the area. (3 times)

2   Knead the gluteals using deep movements. (3 times)

3   Move to the stride standing position and perform double-handed kneading. (3 times)

4   With hands placed at right angles to the wrist and palms both facing each other, apply hacking to the area with fast, light finger movements which flick the skin.

5   Apply beating to the gluteals, clenching the hands into tight fists and hitting the area rhythmically. This can be performed slowly or quickly depending on the response required. Move the hands from shoulder height and place them alternately on the gluteal and back at the starting position. The area is usually covered with a towel to take some of the blows.

6   Pound the gluteals, with the hands held loosely closed, each hand strikes the area alternately in rapid

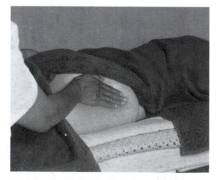

Gluteals and buttocks massage step 1

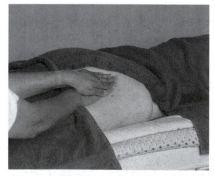

Gluteals and buttocks massage step 2

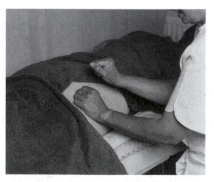

Gluteals and buttocks massage step 5

Tip

In some cases the massage may be performed on top of fabric. For example tapotement manipulations may be performed on the buttock region, with briefs still on, for modesty reasons, if the client is embarrassed. Or a towel can be placed there to receive some of the pressure, if the client is not too well built but wants the movements to be carried out.

succession. This is a very stimulating movement usually used over adipose tissue.

7   Apply clapping to the gluteals. Form cup shapes with the hands and strike the area rhythmically causing a hollow sound. Again, this movement is used over adipose tissue.

8   To complete the massage of the buttocks and gluteals, perform effleurage over the area.

9   Move to the other side of the client, and repeat the routine on the other side.

Back massage

The client should be in lying in the prone position with pillows under the abdomen and the front of the ankles. The client can either rest their forehead on a rolled-up towel or turn their head sideways, with their arms tucked down by their sides.

1   In the walk standing position, effluerage up the back from the sacrum, splitting the hands at the scapula and massaging as far as the deltoid muscles. Slide your hands back down the same route to the starting position. Repeat the effleurage movement covering the trapezius muscle, with the movement ending firmly in the supra-clavicular glands. Slide hands back down the same route. Commence the final movements from the sacrum on the medial borders massaging into the axilla glands before returning. This movement should cover the whole of the back region. (Repeat 6 times)

2   Working from the scapula to the sacrum in three channels on either side of the spine, perform alternate kneading (3 times).

3   Again working in three channels down either side of the spine, this time perform reinforced kneading (ironing). (3 times)

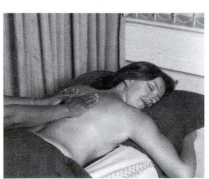

Back massage step 1

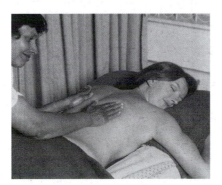

Back massage step 2

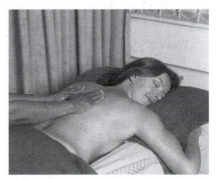

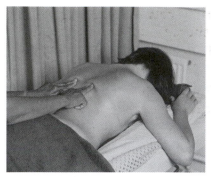

Back massage step 5

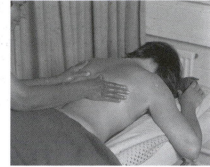

Back massage step 6

4 Place the thumbs in the posterior aspect of the shoulders and thumb knead along the trapezius muscle to the base of the neck. (6 times)

5 Finger knead down both sides of the spine. (3 times)

6 Perform thumb frictions down either side of the spine and then around the scapula. (3 times)

7 In the stride standing position, perform wringing to lateral walls around the back. (3 times)

8 Carry out pick up to the lateral walls around the back. (3 times)

9 Apply skin rolling to the lateral walls around the back. (3 times)

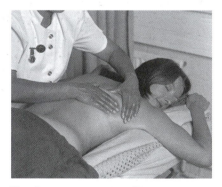

Back massage step 7

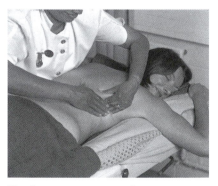

Back massage step 8

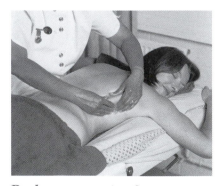

Back massage step 9

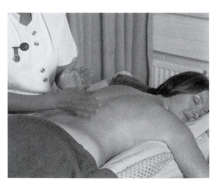

Back massage step 10

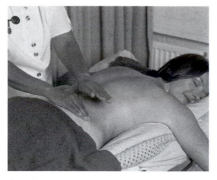

Back massage step 11

10   In the walk standing position, perform hacking to the back. Always ensure that there is sufficient tissue for this manipulation and take care to avoid the spine and any other bony areas. (3 times)

11   Perform cupping/clapping. (3 times)

12   Complete the massage with effleurage.

Aftercare

Once you have completed the body massage, you should take care to ensure that any remaining massage medium is removed with a clean towel or soft tissues before the client gets off the massage couch. You should pay particular attention to the feet, because if there is any excess oil remaining, the client could slip.

You should cover the client with a towel and allow them to rest for a few minutes to allow the circulation to return to normal. This should prevent the client from feeling faint or light-headed. Either while they are resting or once they have rested, you should discuss any aftercare which will compliment the massage. This can include healthy eating and exercise tips, in particular any exercise that could help to improve any postural problems the client may have.

It is important to advise the client to rest for a few hours once they get home. They should be advised not to eat a large or heavy meal but to drink plenty of fluids. The reason for this being that as their circulation continues to return to normal, the blood vessels will constrict resulting in the need to pass water more frequently. An increase in fluid intake is important to avoid dehydration.

Knowledge review – massage techniques and procedures

1 What are the five classifications of massage movements?

2 State the benefits of each type.

3 List the type of manipulations that are included in petrissage movements.

4 Explain the difference between hacking and pounding.

5 What is the commercially acceptable time for:

   a a full body massage

   b an arm massage

   c a back massage

   d neck and chest massage

6 What types of advice would you give a client regarding aftercare?

Modifications to massage treatments

7

Learning objectives

This chapter covers the following:

- **reasons for adapting massage treatments**
- **mechanical treatments**

This chapter details various ways in which massage techniques can be adapted in response to client requirements and limitations. There are many reasons why you may wish to adapt your massage, and these will usually become evident during the course of the pre-treatment consultation. This chapter also introduces basic sports massage and mechanical treatments.

Reasons for adapting massage treatments

Throughout this book is has been stressed that massage should be adapted according to the client's needs and requirements. You should try to gain as much information as possible during the pre-treatment consultation, but you should also continue to solicit feedback throughout the massage in terms of depth of massage, etc. Massage should be adapted because of the physical characteristics or abilities of the client or because of the purpose of the massage.

Adapting massage to various clients

Certain groups of clients will present different problems which will cause you to adapt the usual massage routine.

Physical ability

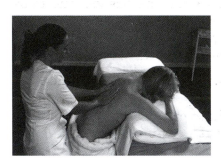

Adapting back massage for client who can't lie down

Tip

Watch your posture! If the client is significantly lower than your hip level, try to sit whenever possible.

The client usually lies on a couch when being massaged, but in some instances this may not be possible. This does not mean that massage cannot be performed but rather the massage procedure would need to be adapted to suit the client's ability.

If a client cannot manage to get onto the massage couch or has problems lying down, for example due to infirmity, it is possible to perform massage on most areas with the client in a chair supported by pillows. From a sitting position, the client's hands and arms, neck, shoulders and chest area, and feet and legs can be massaged easily. The feet and legs can additionally be supported by a stool and pillows.

Clients who are wheelchair-bound may be able to be transferred onto a hydraulically controlled couch. If this is not possible, they can be still treated in their wheelchair as described above.

Many heavily pregnant women do not feel secure being massaged on a couch. If she sits in a low back chair or stool, her hands and arms, feet and legs and neck, shoulders and chest can all be massaged from the sitting position. A full back massage can also be carried out if she remains sitting in the chair but leans in over a couch onto pillows for support.

If a pregnant woman has a massage on the couch, but is too heavily pregnant to lie in the prone position, a back massage can be carried out either as described above, or she can lie on her side on the couch, with her top leg bent at a right angle and with her top arm, elbow bent, palm down, placed near the cheek area. She should be supported by pillows so she will not feel she could roll off.

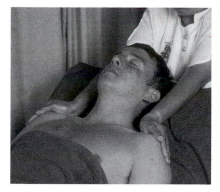 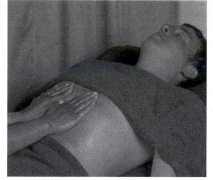 

Male massage

Massage for male clients

If the client is male, massage is usually performed with greater depth, using all of your body weight. This is because male skin tends to be thicker and tougher, the subcutaneous layers contain little fat, the tissues tend to be firmer and the muscles are often resilient and toned. It is also advisable to avoid massaging the lower stomach and the upper inner thigh area (femoral triangle).

Usually an oil lubricant is needed to massage male clients, because they tend to be more hairy. This ensures that your hands glide over the body without causing any pain. If the client is very hairy, it may be better to use talc.

Obese clients

When carried out on an obese client, massage movements should be heavy, deep and quite vigorous and applied in a brisk fashion. The main manipulations applied are deep kneading, wringing, picking up, hacking, clapping, and where there is plenty adipose tissue, pounding and beating. This helps to mobilise the fat deposits. However, you should be careful because it is more difficult to assess the muscle tone and sensitivity in obese clients and excessively heavy movements can cause pain in fatty areas.

Purposes of massage

To relieve gravitational oedema

It is extremely important to ensure that any oedema is non-medical before carrying out a massage treatment. A good way to test this is to press the swollen area. If the oedema is non-medical, the indentation from the pressure will slowly fill with fluid again, leaving the skin cool and pale. If the oedema is medical, do not give a massage and advise the client to seek medical advice. If you are unsure of the cause of the oedema, ask the client to seek medical advice.

Clients susceptible to this condition are those who are on their feet for long periods of time and also those who drink a lot of tea and coffee. The aim of this massage is to direct the movement of fluid to the lymph glands for dispersal. Often clients with oedema tend to have swollen hands, and their feet and ankles also appear puffy.

The best way to massage a client with this type of condition is to ensure the affected area that is being massaged is slightly raised. For example, if the condition affects the leg, it should be raised above the groin area and supported by pillows. If it is the arm, it should be raised higher than the axillae. The most effective manipulations are effluerage and kneading movements. Start to massage the area from the proximal end of the limb and using the two manipulations, effluerage and kneading, squeeze up the whole length of the limb, working slowly and covering all of the area, section by section, working towards the lymph gland.

Female clients may find that their abdomen, legs, hands, and in some instances their face, swell before menstruating. This is usually caused by abnormal water retention which tends to grossly distend the thighs, hips and abdomen. Where the navel distends, the skin appears shiny and in some instances the fluid in the tissue ripples when the client moves. This condition would contraindicate massage, and you should advise the client to seek medical advice.

To relieve aches and pains

The client will normally identify where they have a particular ache or pain, and providing there is no medical condition, the therapist can concentrate on that particular area by applying lots of deep pressure whilst applying effluerage, deep frictions, petrissage and ironing movements.

To relieve stiff joints

As with aches and pains, it is advisable to check that there is no medical reason why the joint is stiff before commencing the massage. The muscles around the stiff joint should be massaged quite vigorously, with effleurage, deep frictions and finger kneading applied to the joint itself.

To relieve contracted muscles

For this type of condition, you should perform deep, slow movements such as stroking, kneading and petrissage. This will help to stretch and relax the muscles. On no account should any percussion movements be applied.

To aid muscle tone

Untoned and flabby muscles may be a result of ageing or weight loss. These type of muscles have usually lost their elasticity. Brisk manipulations are required to stimulate and nourish the muscles that require toning. This can be performed by applying kneading, vibrations, clapping and hacking movements to the area.

To benefit cellulite

This condition is difficult to reduce or remove even when the client is dieting and exercising. The aim of massage is to try and soften and reduce the fatty adipose tissue. Heavier manipulations such as kneading, picking up, hacking, cupping, beating and pounding are required. They should be applied deeply and briskly.

To improve scarring

It is only advisable to massage scar tissue once it is more than nine months old. If it is 'younger' than this, although it may appear healed, the healing process continues in the underlying structures. Massage to this area should consist of manipulations which lift the scar tissue away from the structures underneath. Oil is the best lubricant to use as it allows the skin to stretch more.

To promote relaxation

Achieving a relaxing massage simply involves avoiding/omitting all stimulating movements, such as percussion. You should concentrate on effleurage, stroking, kneading and ironing. These should be performed slowly, rhythmically and firmly with deep pressure being applied. The most beneficial areas to work on are the back and neck areas.

Neuromuscular technique

This technique is usually incorporated into a general massage and is applied to tension nodules/areas of tension. It is important to ensure that the muscles are warmed up first. Using the fingers or thumbs, identify the tense and nodular areas. Using the thumbs (knuckles or elbows), hold the point with deep pressure for up to 90 seconds until the area starts to become less painful. Once the pain starts to ease off, repeat the process. It is better if the client can relax as much as possible while the technique is carried out. This may be difficult due to the pain so the client should be encouraged to do some deep breathing.

To aid stimulation

When the primary aim of a massage is to invigorate the client, you should use quick light manipulations. These will mainly be percussion movements with some petrissage movements such as wringing, picking up and rolling, together with very brisk stroking movements. Stimulating massages are beneficial for clients who complain of a lack of energy and a feeling of debilitation. This type of massage should leave them feeling refreshed and revitalised.

Different massage techniques can be employed dependent on the situation, for example pre-event massage is usually carried out prior to some form of exercise, post-event massage is carried out after exercise has taken place and neuromuscular massage techniques are used to disperse tension nodules.

Pre-event massage (sports massage)

The aim of this type of massage is to:

- help the body to respond well to the demands brought about by increased activity
- facilitate maximum performance.

When muscles are working, an increased supply of oxygen and nutrients are required as muscular activity requires a great deal of energy. It is essential that warm-up and stretching exercises are performed prior to any form of exercise as the body systems are slowly brought up to a peak level, and therefore maximum performance can be obtained. Massage will help to obtain these effects, but under no account must it be used as a substitute for exercise. Massage improves the flexibility and extensibility of muscles, increases blood and nutrient supply to the muscles and helps to maintain and increase joint mobility,

This type of massage, which usually lasts about 10 minutes in each area, is performed lightly and quite briskly. It is a stimulating massage applied to parts of the body that are going to be exercised. The types of movement are effleurage, kneading, wringing and picking up to the main muscles; muscle rolling and light hacking and cupping to the large muscles. You should always start with brisk effleurage working towards the heart.

Post-event massage (sports massage)

This type of massage must be given as soon as possible after exercise. The muscles can be painful, tender and sore due to the accumulation of waste products in the muscles, and as a result of any injuries incurred during exercise. Post-event massage is used to remove metabolic waste by speeding up the venous and lymphatic supply. This helps to prevent stiffness, relieve tension and increase nutrients and oxygen to the muscles, helping to prevent fatigue.

1   Start post-event massage with light, gentle stroking movements over the muscles to get a feel for the condition of the tissues. For example, areas of tension and tightness, and also to allow the client to identify any painful areas.
2   Perform effleurage, increasing the depth as the muscles relax.
3   Shake the muscles using the flat of the hand.
4   Perform muscle rolling.
5   Once the muscles have started to soften, continue massage using kneading, wringing and picking up.
6   Finish the massage with deep stroking and effleurage.

Mechanical treatments

Mechanical massage can be used to either complement manual massage or as a treatment on its own. There are three main types of mechanical treatments according to the equipment used:

1   gyratory vibrator (G5)
2   percussion vibrator
3   audio sonic vibrator

Gyratory vibrator

The gyratory vibrator is usually used in general body work. As it is quite a heavy treatment, it is more suitable for use on large, bulky and muscular areas. This mechanical massage is usually combined with manual massage

Gyratory vibrators can be either hand-held or floor standing. **Hand-held gyratory vibrators** can be quite heavy to hold so often a floor-standing model is preferred unless the therapist needs to carry it to their clients. Another disadvantage is that there are not many head applicators to choose from. Hand-held vibrators have variable speed control to produce either a deep/relaxing or superficial/stimulating effect.

Hand-held gyratory vibrator

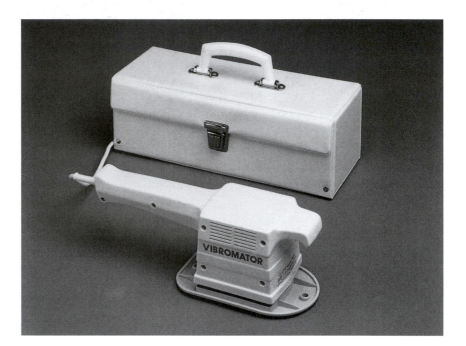

Hand-held gyratory vibrator applicators

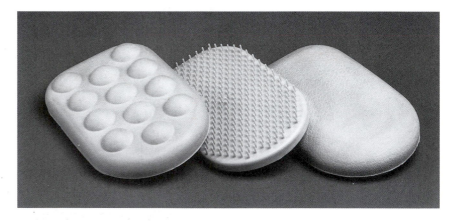

Floor-standing gyratory vibrators are large pieces of machinery supported by a stand. The head is held by the therapist and applied to the client's body. The vibrator operates on a vertical and horizontal plane in a circular movement whilst vibrating up and down, producing a deep massage. This creates the following effects:

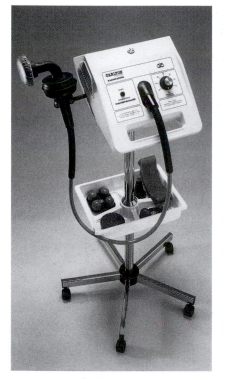

Floor standing gyratory vibrator

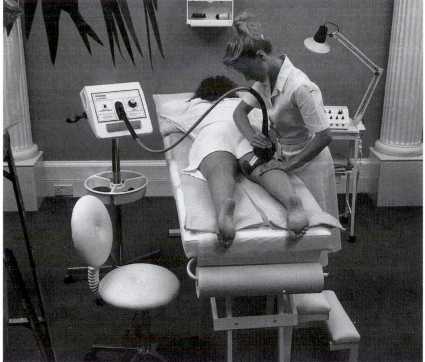

Floor standing gyratory vibrator treatment

- warmth
- increased blood flow, producing an erythema
- relaxed muscles
- increased skin temperature, stimulating the sweat and sebaceous, glands.

Benefits

This is a popular treatment, and the benefits include:

- relaxing tense muscles;
- relieving muscular pain and tension;
- increasing circulation bringing fresh nutrients to the area;
- increasing lymphatic circulation which speeds up the removal of toxins and waste materials;
- improving skin texture by removing the surface dead cells (desquamation);
- stimulating the skins functions and increasing sebaceous activity therefore improving dry skin conditions.

The gyratory vibrator gives a heavy treatment and therefore can assist in improving cellulite as well as helping to disperse fatty deposits, especially if the client is trying to lose weight.

A variety of applicator heads designed to give different effects are available. These are summarised in the table below.

Table 7.1 *Gyratory vibrator heads and their purposes*

Applicator	Illustration	Use	Effect
round sponge applicator		used at the beginning and end of G5 massage on the trunk	effluerage
curved sponge applicator		designed to massage arms and legs	effluerage
round smooth rubber applicator		used on sensitive skin that might be irritated by the sponge	effleurage and petrissage effects
round smooth water massage head		used with either warm or cold water for relaxing or stimulating effects	effleurage and petrissage effects
'egg box' rubber applicator		generally used on bulky muscular areas and fatty tissues such as thighs and buttocks	petrissage
'pronged' rubber applicator		generally used on bulky muscular areas and fatty tissues such as thighs and buttocks	petrissage
'football' rubber applicator		can be used over the colon to promote peristalsis	petrissage
'spiky' rubber applicator		Stimulates nerve endings and creates a rapid hyperemia. Removes surface dead skin cells therefore improving dry skin conditions	tapotement
'lighthouse' rubber applicator		excellent for nodules on upper trapezius, either side of the spine and around the knees	friction

Preparation and procedure

- The attachments should be washed before and after treatment in warm soapy water to remove any talc, dead skin cells and sebum. They should be dried and sanitised in an ultraviolet cabinet. Disposable protective attachment coverings can be used.

- When preparing the treatment area you should cover the couch with clean towels, check all general electrical safety precautions and select applicator attachments.

- Prior to treatment you should ensure that a full consultation, including identifying any possible contraindications, has been carried out and an appropriate treatment plan has been agreed. Ensure that the client has removed all jewellery and check that they are well-supported on the treatment couch. Explain the sensation and demonstrate the noise from the machine to the client.

- Sanitise your own hands and clean and apply talcum powder to the client's skin over the area to be treated.

- The order of treatment is usually: arms, abdomen, front of legs, back of legs, gluteals, back.

- Select the appropriate heads and secure the attachments. Switch the machine on at the mains and then on the machine itself. Test and demonstrate the machine to the client on your forearm.

- Commence the treatment with effleurage applicators. Always use long sweeping strokes in the direction of the lymphatic and venous flow. When massaging the limbs, apply effleurage strokes towards the trunk in one direction. Pressure should be adapted according to muscle bulk. Apply 4–6 strokes to cover the whole area being treated. Always use one hand to lead or follow the applicator head to soothe the skin.

- When changing applicator heads always switch off the machine. Always keep parts of the client's body which are not being treated covered with clean towels.

- Commence petrissage application at the upper treatment part and descend in a circular kneading motion. Lift and glide the tissues under the applicator head with your free hand. A mild erythema can usually be seen on the skin.

Application to body

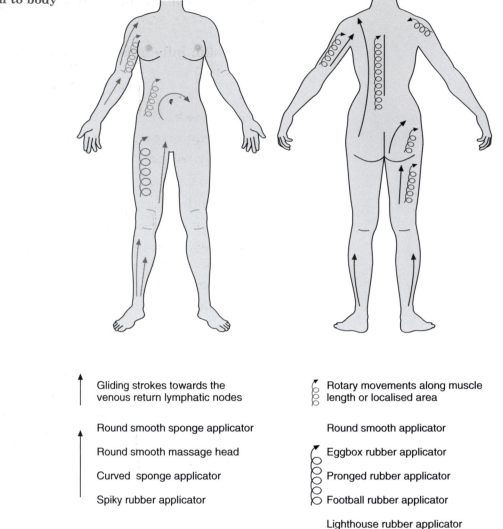

↑ Gliding strokes towards the venous return lymphatic nodes	Rotary movements along muscle length or localised area
Round smooth sponge applicator	Round smooth applicator
Round smooth massage head	Eggbox rubber applicator
Curved sponge applicator	Pronged rubber applicator
Spiky rubber applicator	Football rubber applicator
	Lighthouse rubber applicator (used on upper fibres of trapezius muscle)

Tip

Bruising can result from a too-heavy application or an incorrect choice of applicator head for the treatment area.

- Friction applications are usually applied to small localised areas such as the upper fibres of the trapezius (to relieve tension), either side of the spine (to induce relaxation) and around the knees (to alleviate stiffness). The application is in one direction, in a flowing stroke similar to effleurage.
- Always finish the massage with the effleurage applicators.
- Switch the machine off.
- Complete the client's record card.
- Wash applicators and sanitise.
- Manual massage may be applied to soothe the skin following treatment.

All of the following conditions contraindicate use of the gyratory vibrator:

- skin inflammation/broken skin
- highly vascular skin
- varicose veins
- excessively hairy areas
- bony areas/thin clients
- hypersensitive skin
- recent fractures
- senile skin
- skin tags and moles
- treatment over abdomen during pregnancy and menstruation
- thrombosis or phlebitis
- crêpey skin
- acute back problems.

Audio sonic vibrator

This is a small piece of hand-held machinery suitable for localised areas. This treatment is less stimulating to the skin surface, as it penetrates more deeply into the tissues, making it more suitable for sensitive areas.

Audio sonic vibrator

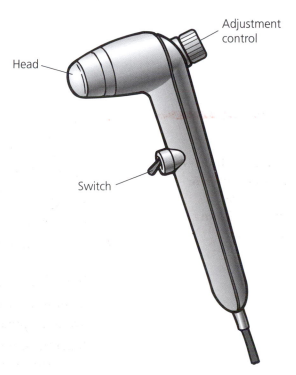

Adjustment control

Head

Switch

The audio sonic vibrator is particularly effective for relaxing tension nodules. When applied to the body, the sensation is very slight, although it penetrates very deeply into the tissues. This is because it uses sound waves created by an electromagnet. When the current is passing forward, the coil in the machine moves forward; when the current passes backward, the coil passes backward. The applicator head is therefore passing forward and backward as the coil compresses and decompresses the skin tissues alternately.

Benefits

- increasing circulation, bringing fresh nutrients and removing waste products;
- produces an erythema improving the skin's colour;
- raises skin temperature promoting relaxation and relieving tension;
- relieves pain;
- aids desquamation improving skin condition.

Preparation and procedure

- The applicator heads should be washed in warm water with a detergent and disinfected with antiseptic.
- Ensure the client is well-supported on the massage couch.
- Explain the treatment to the client and ask the client to remove all jewellery.
- Check for contraindications.
- Cleanse area to be treated.
- Apply lubricant to the area – talc for oily skin, cream for dry to normal skin.
- Select the appropriate head and switch the machine on.
- Test the machine on yourself (forearm).
- Using a circular motion or straight lines cover all the area.
- Apply for 5 to 15 minutes until erythema is present.
- Remove the massage medium from the skin.
- Complete the client's record card.
- Wash applicator heads and sanitise.
- Manual massage may be applied to soothe the skin following treatment.

All of the following conditions contraindicate use of the audio sonic vibrator:

- skin disorders and diseases
- infected skin
- bony areas
- migraines/headaches if applying to face and neck area.

Percussion vibrator

This piece of machinery is hand-held. The applicator head taps up and down on the skin, and the force can be increased and decreased. A variety of heads can be used, for example sponge applicator for effleurage effects and spike for tapotement effects. Percussion vibrators are used mainly on the face, neck and shoulder area. Treatment times vary from 5 to 15 minutes.

Percussion vibrator

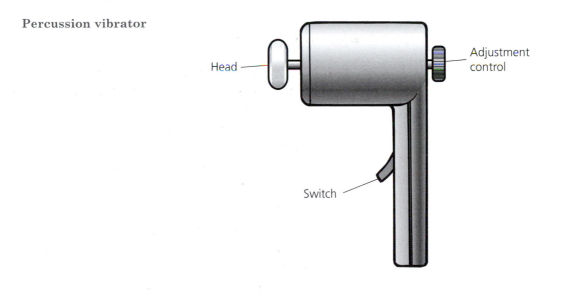

Knowledge review – modifications to massage treatments

1   What areas should be avoided when massaging a male client?

2   How would you adapt the massage routine for the following conditions:
   - gravitational oedema
   - obese clients

3   What massage manipulations would you use to produce:
   - relaxing massage
   - stimulating massage

4   How would you adapt a back massage for a pregnant woman, if she could not lie on her tummy?

5   State three effects of G5.

6   List six contraindications to G5 treatment.

7   What are the effects of the following application heads?
   - 'egg box' rubber application
   - spiky rubber application
   - lighthouse rubber application

8   State two effects of the audio sonic vibrator.

9   List two contraindications to audio sonic treatments.

Baby massage

8

In the last chapter we looked at ways of adapting massage to suit a range of clients. In this chapter we look at an extreme example of adaptation with baby massage.

This chapter introduces you to the theory and techniques of baby massage from the practitioner's perspective and covers baby massage preparation, contraindications, massage procedure, oils and case studies. Further study is required before carrying out or instructing parents in baby massage.

Baby massage has seen a dramatic increase in popularity in the Western world in recent years, becoming extremely popular in health centres, clinics and GPs' surgeries. Although it has only recently started to be practised in the West, it has been popular for hundreds of years in countries like India, Africa and Pakistan.

The power of massage is vastly underestimated. On the whole, we do not realise how much we rely on the sense of touch, and although we recognise massage as a pleasurable experience, its true effects are often overlooked. We learn a great deal by touch, especially in the early years and we need physical contact throughout our whole lives in order to feel loved and accepted. The lightest of touches can convey understanding, sympathy and reassurance.

It is intuitive to stroke and rub the abdomen when pregnant. Touch is the first major sense to develop in the human embryo. A foetus which is only 6 weeks old already responds to touch. In a sense, baby massage begins during the birth process when the strong contractions of labour stimulate the baby's respiratory, digestive, nervous and hormonal systems assisting them to start and begin functioning. Once born, it is natural to stroke a baby to promote sleep or calm them when they are distressed.

Baby massage is very rewarding and an excellent way for you to extend your massage skills, either by teaching parents the skills or by actually massaging babies in special centres. Babies who are deprived of touch can suffer from a sense of loss, isolation, anxiety and a feeling of being unloved, and baby massage is increasingly being regarded as an essential skill in parenthood.

Very light massage can be carried out from the first week after birth. It is most often carried out by the parents and can help facilitate a special bond between the parent and the baby, as both parties adjust to this new situation. Stroking and massaging babies is believed to help them to grow stronger. This is because massage can help to encourage better feeding, and induce relaxation which in turn encourages improved sleep and helps to calm anxiety, improve colic and digestive problems, improve dry skin and eczema complaints and also help with development of awareness, co-ordination and growth patterns.

Benefits of baby massage

In addition to enhancing the loving bond between parent and child, relaxing the parent and baby, and helping to strengthen and regulate the body's systems, massage can also have beneficial effects on feeding, sleep, colic and digestion, and skin complaints.

Feeding

Massaging the baby has been shown to help babies suckle better, mainly because they feel relaxed and contented. This in turn helps to improve feeding patterns and helps to establish a routine. There is not only improvement during the feed given to baby following the massage, but improvement in the long term as well.

Sleep

After massage sleep is usually very deep and will sometimes last many hours, as the baby will feel relaxed and quite contented. It is best to establish a routine where massage is carried out each day at the same time.

Colic and digestion

Massage stimulates the whole body, and each of the systems improve.

Massage assists the organs to function better: blood, lymph, skin and muscles are stimulated to work more efficiently. The digestive system can be improved by massaging the abdomen, but massaging the abdomen and the chest areas should be avoided until the baby is at least one month old. Using your fingertips to gently massage around the baby's abdomen in a clockwise direction – stroking along the colon – will help to relieve colic.

Skin complaints

Using oil to massage a baby will help to improve their often dry skin. Plain almond oil is good because it is fine and easily absorbed. Vegetable oils, like grapeseed oil, can also be used. Avoid nut-based oil as many babies are allergic to nuts. If the baby suffers from cradle cap, a little almond oil massaged on the head will feed the skin and gently lift off the scales.

Preparation

Before a nap or after bath time and before bed is a good time for baby massage, if you want to promote sleep and relaxation. Whatever time you practise baby massage, make sure it is always at least 30 minutes after their last feed. It is especially important to make sure the aromatherapy environment is sage when carrying out baby massage.

Tip

Initially, it is advisable for the therapist to demonstrate to parents /carer the massage technique with the baby on the floor.

Tip

Oiling and stretching the baby's body can help the baby to grow stronger, encourage better feeding, deeper sleep and relief from colic.

Checklist:

- Ensure that the room is warm.
- Wash and dry your hands and make sure they are warm.
- Remove your jewellery, otherwise you may catch and scratch the baby's skin.
- Check the lighting is neither too dim nor too bright.

If possible, carry out the massage either with the baby on the floor, on a towel or on your lap. Make sure there is plenty of support to keep them from falling. Ensure there is always plenty of time so the massage is not rushed. Baby massage times can vary from 5 to 30 minutes, depending on the reactions of the baby. Although baby massage can be carried out on babies from one week after birth, as the baby grows they will start to take an active part in the massage responding by kicking, wriggling and gurgling.

Here are a few points to take into consideration before carrying out the massage technique:

- If the baby was born by caesarean, it is thought to be beneficial to massage as frequently as possible as the baby would not have experienced the strong contractions of labour.
- If the baby was delivered using forceps, you may find their head very sensitive to touch. If this is the case, avoid this area until the sensitivity has passed.
- If a baby was born with the umbilical cord around their neck during birth, this can also lead to sensitivity. Again, it is best to avoid massaging the area until the sensitivity has passed.
- In some cases, it is better just to hold premature babies at first, depending on how premature they are. Babies who have received gentle stroking and fingertip massage to the face and body, tend to gain weight more quickly as this improves their ability to suck. This can also benefit the mother who has missed out on the bonding time when the baby is in the incubator.

Contraindications

Contraindications to performing the massage are:

- skin diseases and disorders
- vomiting

- fever
- high temperature
- appearance of being unsettled.

Massage techniques

The main massage movements used in baby massage are:

- effleurage or stroking
- petrissage
- gentle stretching

Effleurage

This movement is soothing and relaxing. It helps to increase circulation as well as linking other movements together. The stroke should always be applied lightly but firmly and applied by fingers rather than the palms as the area is very small.

Petrissage

These movements include kneading, lifting and rolling soft tissue. They tend to be carried out by the fingers and thumbs and can help to reduce tension, increase the absorption of nutrients and stimulate the elimination of waste.

Gentle stretching

This must be carried out very gently. It helps to increase joint mobility, maintain flexibility of joints and encourage the development of strength and suppleness.

Massage procedure

Stroking movements are mainly used, as the baby's body is small.

1   Begin on the front of the body. Warm oil in your clean hands, before applying it to the baby using long strokes. Starting from the toes, up the legs, onto the tummy, then up onto the chest around the shoulders, down the arms, to the finger tips, then all the way back

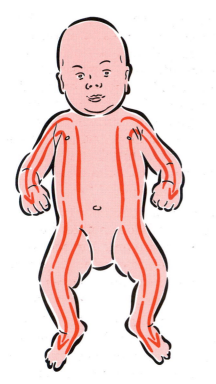

Baby massage step 1

from the finger tips to the toes, taking care to avoid the face. Do not apply too much oil to the hands as babies tend to rub their eyes and this could irritate them.

2 Massage using effluerage movements from the belly button up to the sternum and back down. This helps conditions such as coughs, colds and asthma.

3 Massage the tummy, first up and down the torso, then with fingertips, go clockwise around the naval. Massaging the colon will help prevent colic, wind and constipation.

4 Effleurage the arm. Holding the baby's hand in yours, gently stretch the arm covering the whole area to up around the shoulders. Apply a little more oil around the neck area, if needed, as babies can become chapped here through dribbling. Uncurl the hand and gently stroke the palm and the back of the hand using your thumbs. Rotate each finger slowly and carefully. Finish with a light squeeze of the hand. Repeat on the other arm and hand.

5 Hold the foot in one hand and very gently stretch the leg. Effleurage the leg from the foot to the groin and then back down. Stroke the foot from the toes to the ankles, around the ankle bone and stroke underneath the foot using the pads of your thumbs. Gently massage the toes between the thumb and first finger using a rotating movement (kneading). At this point it is

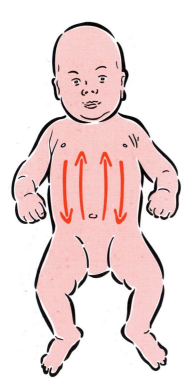

Baby massage step 2

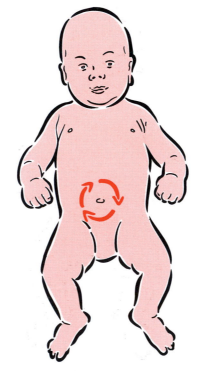

Baby massage step 3

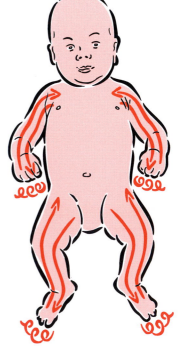

Baby massage step 4 and 5

beneficial to use some reflexology pressure points. The big toe represents the head and neck area, the second and third the eyes (this can help if the baby suffers from sticky eye) and the fourth and fifth toes represent the ears (which can be affected when baby is teething and also will help to prevent glue ear). Each toe can then be rotated individually taking great care. Finish off by finding the dimple on the sole of the foot and applying a small circular movement with your thumb. This is the solar plexus, and the movement has a calming effect. Repeat the procedure on the other leg and foot.

6   The face may be included. Always remember to stroke the head away from the eyes so oil does not get into them. Apply stroking movements up onto the cheeks, circling around the eye area – taking care not to get too close to the eyes – stroking down the nose, across the forehead and then stroke the top and back of the head.

The ears may be included by massaging them between the thumb and first finger, with a kneading movement, gently covering the lobe. Massaging the face and head can help prevent congestion and a stuffy nose. It is also very relaxing and can help the baby to sleep if overtired or unwell.

7   Turn the baby over onto their tummy.

8   Stroke from the ankle up to the buttocks then proceed to the back area up to the neck. It is important to take care to avoid the spine at all times.

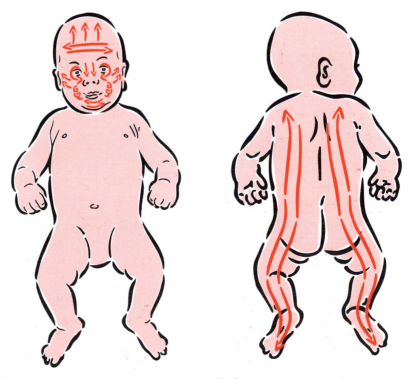

Baby massage step 6   Baby massage step 8

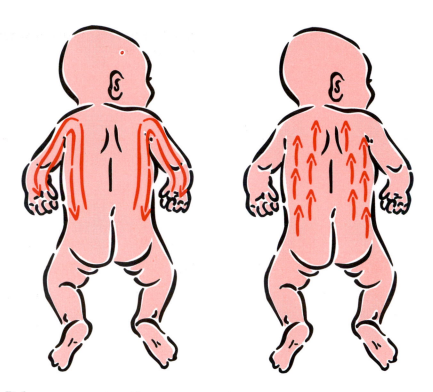

Baby massage step 10   Baby massage step 12

9   Effleurage the back up to the shoulders, across the
     shoulders, down the back of the arms, then back to the
     starting position.

10   Stroke over and around each of the buttocks in an
     anti-clockwise direction. Massaging the back and
     buttock area will help constipation and wind, as well
     as being extremely relaxing.

11   Effleurage the back from the buttocks, up to the neck
     and back. Repeat several times.

12   To finish stroke slowly, one hand following the other
     down the whole of the back. When one hand gets to the
     base of the back, gently lift off and then start again,
     each time decreasing the pressure and the pace.

13   Wrap baby in a warm towel to finish.

Aftercare

Parents and carers should always remove all lubricants
from the skin, especially if the baby is to have a bath. Avoid
sunlight after massage. Always give the baby plenty of
fluids and keep them warm. Allow the baby to sleep.

Parents and carers could massage their baby everyday, if
they so wish. As the baby becomes older, it could perhaps be

reduced to once or twice a week. It is entirely up to the parent and the baby.

Oils

The following vegetable oils are suitable for use on babies:

Table 8.1 *Vegetable oils*

Oil	Indication
almond oil	particularly good as it is soothing and calming. Suitable for all skin types
sunflower oil	very light oil containing Vitamin E. Particularly good for dry skin type
grapeseed oil	a gentle emollient which helps to retain moisture. Suitable for all skin types
olive oil	excellent source of Vitamin E. Particularly suitable for dry and inflamed skins, as it has soothing properties

In addition, a number of essential oils are also suitable for use on babies and infants over six months old.

Table 8.2 *Essential oils*

Oil	Description	Properties
lavender	very soothing and relaxing, helps to settle the infant.	sedative for restless babies and children. Soothes skin disorders such as eczema. Good for colic or constipation
	can be used either blended in with massage oil, or in the bath. Use only in low concentrations	stimulant for chest congestion. Can be beneficial for relief of colds, bronchial

Table 8.2 *(continued)*

Oil	Description	Properties
		conditions and asthma. Excellent antiseptic. Heals minor burns, disinfects cuts and sores, relieves insect bites and stings
camomile	gentle and soothing, particularly well suited for young children. Use only in an extremely low concentration Blends well with lavender and reinforces its sedative nature	excellent for skin disorders such as eczema, psoriasis and nappy rash. Particularly effective for indigestion, colic and constipation, can be used as an antiseptic, especially good on grazes and skin that is inflamed
mandarin and orange	must be used in extremely low dilutions. Must not be used on sensitive skins and sunlight must be avoided after use. Very light fresh and fruity aroma, children tend to love the smell. When blended with lavender it reinforces its sedative powers.	good to use for colic and indigestion. Helps as a sedative on over-tired and restless infants. Mildly astringent
eucalyptus and peppermint		good to use in steamers if the infant is suffering from a chest cold or congestion

Case studies

Case study 1

GENDER: Female

AGE: 6 months

REASON FOR TREATMENT: Jayne has not been sleeping well for the past month, waking up every two to three hours each night. Jayne has always been a good sleeper from a few weeks old.

FREQUENCY OF VISITS: Daily for the first four days

OUTCOME: First visit: On the first visit Jayne was very unsure of me as we had never met before. I felt at this stage we should not undress her completely, but only massage her feet, legs, arms, hands and face. Jayne did a lot of wriggling, and became very distressed if her mum moved away. She only seemed to relax when we started on her feet which she seemed to enjoy a lot.
Throughout the massage I was instructing her mum on the procedure, so this eventually could be carried out each evening after her bath or before bedtime.

Second treatment: Jayne was still a little unsure of me, but she was not distressed. This time, we massaged the same areas as we did previously but managed to include the abdomen.

Third treatment: Jayne seemed pleased to see me, was quite happy to be undressed, and the full massage routine was carried out with Jayne's mum assisting. She seemed to particularly like having her feet massaged. At the end of the massage, Jayne was sound asleep and carried to her bed.

Fourth treatment: Jayne was thrilled to see me this time. Her mum carried out the whole routine with me supervising. Again Jayne fell asleep and was carried to her bed.

GENERAL COMMENTS: After the first visit she became very restless and there was no improvement in her sleep pattern. After the second session she was more content and her sleeping improved – she only awoke twice in the night. The last two sessions proved to be a success. Jayne slept through the night without waking up at all, and on the last session, had to be woken up as she had slept until the afternoon, which had never happened before.

I have since spoke to Jayne's mum who still massages her every evening after her bath and just before bed, not always carrying out a full massage, but always including her feet. Jayne is still continuing to sleep through the night with no disturbances.

Case study 2

GENDER: Male

AGE: 3 months

REASON FOR TREATMENT: Teething problems which are affecting his sleeping pattern.

FREQUENCY OF VISIT: Daily over a five day period.

OUTCOME: First visit: Matthew was very distressed. He had more teeth coming through and was in a great deal of pain. His fist was continually in his mouth, and he was constantly dribbling, cheeks burning and very red. At first we spent time cuddling and stroking and then positioned him in my lap rather than on the floor. We only massaged his legs and feet. He became very upset so I massaged his solar plexus until he calmed down. He seemed to get some relief when massaging his toes.

Second visit: Carried out massage an hour after his final feed just before bed, he was a little calmer than the previous session. We cuddled and played a little before massaging. This time we managed to massage his legs, feet, arms, chest and abdomen. He became quite drowsy and looked content so we decided not to spoil it by putting him on his tummy.

Third visit: The whole massage was carried out and he particularly enjoyed his back massage.

Fourth visit: In the last two sessions, Matthew's mum carried out full massage, while I supervised and assisted. Matthew enjoyed this and there was a lot of eye contact between the two of them. He was very content and relaxed, and towards the end while working on his back he fell into a deep sleep.

GENERAL COMMENT: Over this period of time Matthew was in a lot of pain because of the teething. As the days went on he seemed to get some relief from the massage. During the day his mum would massage his feet if he became unduly upset, as it was found that he would eventually calm down if you massaged his feet especially if she massaged the pressure point for his solar plexus.

Using almond oil as the lubricant meant his skin improved a great deal particularly around the neck area as it was rather chapped from his constant dribbling.

Matthew slept very well after the final two visits and continued to do so, as his mum carried on massaging each evening before bed and whenever he got upset. Even after his bout of teething is over, his mum has decided to continue the massage each evening, as she feels this is their quality time.

Consultation form

Don't forget to carry out a full consultation prior to carrying out any massage. The following is an example of some of the questions that need to be asked of either the parent or carer.

Baby's name: _____

Date of birth: _____

Parents/guardian name: _____

Address and telephone number: _____

Doctor's name and telephone number: _____

Health visitor's name and telephone number: _____

Birth details – type of delivery, weight: _____

Sleep patterns: _____

Eating patterns: _____

Any relevant medical history – recent operations or immunisations, skin disorders, fractures or sprains, cuts, abrasions, skin rashes, allergies, current infections:

_____

_____

_____

_____

_____

_____

Do not forget to get the parent or guardian's signature and record any details of the treatment.

Knowledge review – baby massage

1 State the contraindications to baby massage.

2 Which oils can safely be used to massage a baby?

3 State the main benefits of baby massage.

4 When is the best time to carry out a massage on a baby?

Aromatherapy massage

9

Learning objectives

This chapter covers the following:

- **history**
- **essential oils**
- **carrier or fixed oils**
- **aromatherapy massage**

This chapter introduces both the theory and practical techniques of aromatherapy so that you can provide accurate advice and guidance and carry out suitable treatments.

History

Aromatherapy is a natural therapy using essences of plants. The use of essential oils helps to restore, revive and balance both the mind and the body resulting in a feeling of well-being. Aromatherapy has been used for thousands of years. The first known medical book λ written in 2000 BC refers to a Emperor Kiwati-Ti who studied opium and rhubarb and recognised their properties as we know them today.

Egyptians used aromatic essences to embalm – frankincense, myrrh and cedar wood – and mummify – cinnamon and clove – their dead. They also used 'essential oils' in their religious ceremonies and were the first to use the oils for cosmetic purposes. The ancient Greeks used essences as perfumes, to cure illnesses and in massage. Hippocrates fought the Athens Plague with aromatic fumigations and herbal medicine! The Romans used 'essential oils' for their healing properties, particularly on battle wounds, and the use of aromatic oils is also reported in the Bible, e.g. Jesus Christ is said to have used aromatic oils in healing and Mary Magdalene anointed Jesus' feet with them at the Last Supper.

The Arabs discovered the art of distilling essential oils in 10 AD. The Crusaders brought this knowledge and recipes back to their own country between 10 and 12 AD, and by 13 AD the distillation of plants started and chemical products ensued. Knowledge of aromatics and herbs increased throughout Medieval history and was studied by many physicians. By the eighteenth century essential oils were being used in medicine and by the nineteenth century they were popularly used in the perfume industry.

It is in fact a French chemist named Gattefosse who may be credited as being the real founder of aromatherapy in the early twentieth century. While working in the laboratory, he burnt himself badly with a bunsen burner. He immediately plunged his burnt hand into a vat of lavender oil and inadvertently discovered how quickly the burn healed without leaving a scar or becoming infected. Following this incident, Gattefosse conducted more research into essential oils and published his first book on aromatherapy in 1928.

During WWII, a French doctor, Dr Jean Valnet, began to use essential oils on wounded soldiers. Marguerite Maurey, a biochemist working for a perfumery, introduced massage as a way of getting the oils into the body. And in the 1950s, she introduced aromatherapy to England, when she travelled to London and opened a clinic where the art of aromatherapy was both practised and taught.

Today, many people are looking for alternative methods to help relieve some of the stresses and tensions of modern life. Given that stress is one of the main contributory factors to many diseases and disorders such as high blood pressure and heart disease, aromatherapy has become particularly popular.

Aromatherapists are now found working in hospitals and doctors' surgeries, as well as alternative centres and beauty clinics.

The oils can be used in many ways:

- massage
- inhalation
- steamer
- compresses
- air sprays
- burners
- baths
- lotions/oils
- candles
- foot spas
- hair/skin products
- potpourris

Tip

See later in chapter for aspects of consultation in aromatherapy in relation to the use of essential oils.

Essential oils

An essential oil is an oil present in a flower, fruit, root, leaf, seed, bark or an aromatic plant. Oils are in the form of tiny odoriferous droplets, and it is these droplets that are always changing their chemical composition according to the change of season or time of day. Essential oils have a large range of aromas and colours including red, brown, blue, yellow and green. As well as being used in aromatherapy, essential oils are also found in perfumes, pharmaceuticals and food flavourings. They are largely made up of three elements – carbon, hydrogen and oxygen.

The molecules in essential oils are very small, and this is how they are able to penetrate through the skin and into the blood stream. Even though the components are individually relatively simple in structure, an oil can be made up of hundreds of components, some only being present in small amounts. It could be that it is these trace components that have the therapeutic properties and that helps to explain why chemically reproduced oils may smell very similar but do not have the same therapeutic properties.

Although essential oils have a very simple molecular structure, the active constituents which make up the oil make it complex. These active constituents work **synergistically**, they work much more powerfully and effectively when combined with other oils.

Tip

Oils from the same botanical family group blend well together.

Properties of essential oils

Essential oils:

- mix with mineral oil and vegetable oil
- do not mix with water or alcohol
- have an odour
- evaporate
- are not greasy to touch
- are volatile, although the extent of the volatility varies according to whether the essential oils are **top**, **middle** or **base** note.

Top note

Top note essential oils are the most volatile. They have a sharp aroma and a highly stimulating effect. They are absorbed into the skin very quickly, last on the skin for about 24 hours and are used to stimulate the mind and body.

Top notes are obtained from citrus fruits:

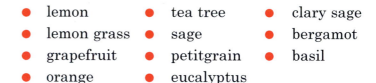

- lemon
- lemon grass
- grapefruit
- orange
- tea tree
- sage
- petitgrain
- eucalyptus
- clary sage
- bergamot
- basil

Middle note

Middle note essential oils are moderately volatile and last on the skin for about two to three days. They are used to help bodily functions. Middle notes are usually obtained from flowers and herbs:

- rosemary
- pine
- black pepper
- lavender
- juniper
- fennel
- geranium
- marjoram
- melissa
- camomile
- cypress

Base note

Base note essential oils are known as fixatives as they 'hold back' the fast evaporation of the top note essential oils. They have the slowest evaporation rate and last for about seven days, as they are absorbed very slowly into the skin. Their effect is soothing on the mind and body.

Base notes are obtained from woods and resins which have a rich, heavy aroma with a relaxing and sedating effect:

- ylang-ylang
- frankincense
- myrrh
- sandal wood
- patchouli
- ginger
- rose
- ginger
- jasmine

Storing essential oils

Tip

Always buy from a reputable supplier.

Essential oils all have different shelf lives and some last longer than others. However, if oils are not stored correctly, they will lose their therapeutic properties. Essential oils should always be stored in a cool, dark place away from direct sunlight. Exposure to light and extremes of temperature can damage the oil's properties. The storage bottles should be dark in colour to prevent light damage, air tight and made of glass. You should never store essential oils in plastic bottles as these are permeable – air may reach the oil and damage it.

Composition of essential oils

Essential oils consist of many chemical components, including:

- terpene
- ester
- ketone
- alcohol
- aldehde
- phenol

It is these chemical components that give the essential oils their specific properties.

Table 9.1 Composition of essential oils

Component	Properties	Where they are found
terpene	antiseptic, antiviral	lemon, peppermint, pine, thyme, tea tree
alcohol	anti-inflammatory, antiseptic, diuretic, stimulates the immune system	thyme, lemon, sandalwood, peppermint, bergamot
ester	anti-inflammatory, antispasmodic, sedative, fungicidal	lemon, rosemary, lavender, bergamot
aldehde	antiseptic, antiviral, anti-inflammatory, sedative	melissa, lemongrass
ketone	helps formation of scar tissue, eases congestion by aiding in flow of mucus	rosemary, peppermint, fennel, camphor, eucalyptus
phenol	antiseptic, antispasmodic, stimulating	thyme, eucalyptus

Methods of extracting essential oils

Enfleurage

Enfleurage is a method using cold fat. A thin layer of fat is spread on a glass frame and fresh flowers that continue to produce essential oils even after they are picked, are put in layers on top of this. The essential oils are absorbed into the fat. The glass frame is then turned, and the flowers fall off to be replaced with new ones. This process is continued for about two months. When the fat has been saturated with essential oil, it is washed in pure alcohol, and the oil passes into the alcohol known as an absolute. The alcohol is then evaporated leaving the pure essential oil. This method has now been superceded by other methods.

Distillation

This is an ancient method, but it is still the most widely-used technique for extracting essential oils from plants. Distillation involves heating the plants with water in a still. Steam is produced which contains the essential oil and it passes into a condenser where the vapour turns into a liquid consisting of water and the essential oils. The essential oil floats on the water, because it is less dense, which allows it to be siphoned off.

This method is usually used to produce lavender, rose and ylang-ylang.

Expression

In expression, a machine is used to crush the rind of the fruit and extract the oil. Years ago, this was extracted by holding a sponge around the rind of the fruit and squeezing until the sponge was filled with oil. Citrus fruits such as lemon and orange are extracted using this method.

Maceration

This method involves dipping plants into hot fat. The process is repeated with fresh supplies of flowers until the fat becomes saturated. The fat is then washed in alcohol which evaporates and leaves the essential oil. This method is rarely used any more.

Solvent

The solvent used is dependent on the source of the essential oils. For flowers, ether, benzine or petroleum is used, while for gums such as rosewood and pine and resins such as myrrh and benzoin, the solvent used is acetone. The plants are covered with a solvent and heated gradually until the essential oil is extracted. The solvent is then filtered, and the dark paste that is left is mixed with alcohol and left to cool. The essential oil dissolves in the alcohol which then evaporates leaving the oil.

Methods of entry of essential oils into the body

Skin

Essential oils can enter the skin via sebaceous glands, sudoriferous glands and hair follicles. Penetration of essential oils into the skin can take up to 100 minutes. Carrier oils, especially acids, alkalis and alcohols, can only pass through to the epidermis as the modular structure is too large for them to penetrate any further. Because essential oils have small molecular structures though, once the oils have entered the skin, they can penetrate through to the dermis, and then pass through to the blood stream via the capillary walls. The blood then transports essential oils around the body.

Respiratory system

Essential oils can be inhaled. They pass through the lung tissue lining, through the capillary walls into the blood stream and are transported around the body.

Olfactory system

Responsible for the sense of smell, the olfactory system is stimulated when we smell something, and the body responds. Volatile essential oils penetrate the olfactory system when inhaled. The olfactory surface is coated with a thin layer of mucus, the oils pass through the mucous membranes and fatty tissues where they stimulate the olfactory nerves and the odour is registered. If the mucous membranes are blocked, for example when you have a cold, substances have difficulty passing through and it is difficult to differentiate smells.

Elimination of essential oils

Essential oils stay in the body for some time, in particular the ones that are in the deeper organs. They are eliminated by a number of methods including perspiration, exhalation and in the urine.

Effects of essential oils

Essential oils can have psychological and physiological effects. Often, the physiological effects can be directly attributed to the mental effects. In many cases, an essential oil can affect both mood and physiology.

Table 9.2 *Psychological effects of essential oils*

Effect	Essential oils
calming	camomile, geranium, juniper, lavender, sandalwood, ylang-ylang, marjoram
uplifting	basil, geranium, lavender, lemon grass, peppermint
soothing	cypress, lavender
energising	marjoram
relaxing	camomile, cypress, sandalwood, ylang-ylang
stimulating	basil, juniper, lemon, lemon grass, rosemary, peppermint
sedative	cedarwood, cypress, lavender, lemon, marjoram, sandalwood, patchouli
revitalising	lemon grass, juniper

Table 9.3 *Physiological effects of essential oils*

Effect	Essential oils
raising body temperature	camphor
lowering body temperature	camomile
increasing circulation	rosemary, eucalyptus, black pepper
lowering blood pressure	lavender
respiratory – decrease muscle spasms	fennel, peppermint, rose, clary sage
respiratory – expectorant effect	eucalyptus, benzoin lemon
sedative effect on nervous system	melissa, lavender, sandalwood, ylang-ylang
stimulating effect on nervous system	lemon, fennel, cinnamon
antispasmodic effect on digestive system	lavender, rosemary, sandalwood
laxative effect	marjoram, rosemary
diuretic effect	juniper, fennel, sandalwood
stimulate oestrogen production	fennel, aniseed, garlic
antibacterial effect	most oils

Safety of essential oils

The majority of essential oils should never be used undiluted. The most common risks of essential oils are:

Toxicity — This is similar to poisoning. If the oil is toxic it could prove to be fatal if taken orally or applied to the skin. Toxicity is a matter of dose which varies according to the persons size, for example a child should have a much lower percentage of essential oils blended in the carrier oil than an adult, and the treatment should be less frequent. Certain oils are **phototoxic** which means that the skin will be more sensitive to the sunlight

Irritation — Irritation to the skin and mucous membrane is most likely.

Sensitisation — This is an allergic reaction to the essential oil. It only requires a small amount to cause a reaction.

Tip

Always keep a record of the oils you use on the client. In the event of a problem such as irritation the therapist can identify the oil involved and make the changes accordingly.

Some essential oils used in aromatherapy massage are contraindicated to certain conditions. If medical consent is given to massage a client suffering from a specific condition, you should check for any associated contraindicated oils.

Conditions with contraindicated oils include:

high blood pressure — avoid rosemary, sage, thyme, hyssop

epilepsy — avoid hyssop, sage and fennel

pregnancy — avoid basil, aniseed, cinnamon, carrot seed, clove, clary sage, cypress, cedar wood, fennel, lemon grass, marjoram, origanum, parsley, peppermint, rose, rosemary, sage and thyme

Bergamot, lemon, orange, lime and angelic should be avoided prior to exposure to sunlight.

Table 9.4 Essential oils for use in aromatherapy massage

Essential oil	Extraction	Uses	Properties	Caution
basil	steam distillation from tops of flowers and leaves	digestive problems, muscular aches and pains, asthma, sinusitis, bronchitis, coughs, irregular periods, anxiety, depression, migraine	antidepressant, antiseptic, expectorant, emmenagoguic, stimulates and clears the mind	may cause irritation and sensitisation, avoid during pregnancy
benzoin	solvent extraction from the resin which is collected from the bark of the tree	nervous tension and exhaustion, muscular aches and pains, respiratory ailments, digestive conditions, dry, chapped skin types, helps expel excess body fluid	nerve sedative, antiseptic, astringent, anti-inflammatory, circulatory, stimulant	can cause sensitisation
bergamot	expressed from the rind	digestive problems, respiratory conditions, urinary infections, stress, anxiety, nervous tension and depression	antiseptic, astringent, laxative diuretic, uplifting, antidepressant, stimulant	avoid contact with strong sunlight after using this oil – photosensitive
black pepper (middle note)	steam distillation of the dried fruit i.e. peppercorns	poor circulation, muscular aches and pains, loss of appetite, nausea, colds and flu, lethargy and mental fatigue	analgesic, antiseptic, antispasmodic, antitoxic, appetite-stimulant, bactericidal, diuretic, laxative, stimulant of nervous, circulatory and digestive systems	use in lowest concentration as it may irritate the skin
camomile (roman) (middle note)	steam distillation of the flowering heads	acne, allergies, boils, burns, eczema, inflamed skin conditions, earache, wounds, menstrual pains, headaches, premenstrual syndrome, nervous tension and other stress related disorders	analgesic, anti-allergenic, anti-inflammatory, antispasmodic, bactericidal, carminative, digestive, emmenagoguic, fungicidal, hepatic and sedative	avoid during the first few months of pregnancy
cedar wood (base note)	steam distillation from the wood	anxiety, nervous tension, eczema, dermatitis, insect repellent	antiseptic, sedative, astringent	do not use during pregnancy. Use low concentrations as it may cause skin irritation

Essential oil	Extraction	Uses	Properties	Caution
clary sage (top note)	steam distillation of the flowering tops and leaves	high blood pressure, muscular aches and pains, respiratory problems, irregular menstruation, premenstrual syndrome, depression, migraine, nervous tension and stress related disorders.	anticonvulsive, antidepressant, antispasmodic, antiseptic, astringent, bactericidal, deodorant, digestive and sedative	not to be used in pregnancy or immediately before or after drinking alcohol
cypress	steam distillation from the twigs, cones and needles	respiratory problems – asthma and bronchitis; menstrual problems and menopause symptoms; oedema, poor circulation, rheumatism	antiseptic, astringent, anti-rheumatic, diuretic, regulates menstrual cycle	emmenagoguic
eucalyptus (top note)	steam distillation of the young leaves and twigs	burns, blisters, chickenpox, measles, cold sores, cuts, insect bites and stings, insect repellant, head lice, skin infections, wounds, arthritis, muscular aches and pains, sprains, poor circulation, cystitis, hay fever, cold and flu, and headaches	analgesic, anti-rheumatic, antiseptic, antiviral, deodorant, diuretic, expectorant, parasiticidal, stimulant and vulnerary	allergy sufferers may need a skin test prior to use
fennel (middle note)	steam distillation from the herb's crushed seeds	digestive problems, constipation, flatulence, cellulite, menstrual/menopausal problems, poor circulation	diuretic properties, circulatory stimulant, antiseptic, tonic, laxative, detoxicant, anti-inflammatory	phototoxic, avoid during pregnancy and with epileptics, only use sweet fennel and not bitter finnel in aromatherapy
frankincense (base note)	steam distillation of the tears of the resin produced by making incisions in the bark	skin care (particularly ageing skin), acne, abscesses, scars, wounds, haemorrhoids, respiratory ailments such as asthma, bronchitis, coughs and catarrah, cystitis, painful	anti-inflammatory, antiseptic, astringent, carminative, digestive, diuretic, emmenagoguic, expectorant, sedative and tonic	as the oil is an emmenagogue do not use in the first few months of pregnancy

Table 9.4 (continued)

Essential oil	Extraction	Uses	Properties	Caution
frankincense (continued)		menstruation, uterine bleeding outside menstruation, premenstrual syndrome, nervous tension and stress related disorders		may irritate sensitive skin
geranium (middle note)	steam distillation of the leaves, stalks and flowers	burns, eczema, head lice, ringworm, cellulite, haemorrhoids, poor circulation, engorgements of the breasts, menopausal problems, premenstrual syndrome, nervous tension and stress related disorders.	antidepressant, anti-inflammatory, antiseptic, astringent, deodorant, diuretic, fungicidal, stimulant of the adrenal cortex, tonic and vulnerary	
ginger (base note)	distillation from dried ground root	digestive, poor circulation, respiratory problems, muscular aches and pains	warming effect on muscular system, stimulant, antiseptic, bactericidal, tonic	use in low concentration, may cause irritation and skin sensitivity
grapefruit	express from fruit peel	respiratory problems, fluid retention, cellulite, depression and nervous exhaustion, acne and oily skin	antiseptic, antitoxic, astringent, stimulant (lymphatic system), bactericidal, diuretic, calming, uplifting antidepressant	this oil oxidises quickly and once this occurs it can cause irritation
jasmine (base note)	solvent extraction of the flower	respiratory problems, menstrual pain, labour pain, depression, effective when used on scarring	relaxing, relieves emotional stress and depression, antiseptic, aids child birth (parturient), expectorant	never use in pregnancy but can be used to help in labour, use in low proportion, very expensive
juniper (middle note)	steam distillation of the crushed, dried berries	poor circulation, fluid retention, weeping eczema, wounds, cellulite, haemorrhoids, arthritic	warming, helps to heal wounds, antiseptic, antispasmodic, astringent, carminative, diuretic, emmenagoguic,	can be a skin irritant, avoid use

Essential oil	Extraction	Uses	Properties	Caution
juniper (continued)		and rheumatic complaints, muscular aches and pains, loss of periods outside pregnancy, painful menstruation, cystitis, premenstrual syndrome nervous tension and stress related disorders	nervine, parasiticidal, sedative and tonic	during pregnancy, very stimulating so use sparingly, avoid with severe kidney disorders
lavender (middle note)	steam distillation from the flowery heads of the plant	headaches, depression, digestive problems, menstrual pain, respiratory problems	antiseptic, balancing, harmonising, promotes healing of burns, wounds and sores, bactericidal, decongestant, sedative, antidepressant, calming, soothing, builds up the immune system, diuretic, antibiotic, warming	avoid in the first part of pregnancy
lemon (top note)	cold compression from the rind of the fruit. A distilled oil is also available	oily skin, acne, boils, warts, chilblains, arthritis, high blood pressure, poor circulation, rheumatism, asthma, sore throats, bronchitis, catarrh, indigestion, colds and flu	antirheumatic, antiseptic, antispasmodic, antitoxic, astringent, carminative, bactericidal, diuretic, hypotensive, insecticidal and tonic	lemon like other citrus fruits is phototoxic
lemon grass (top note)	steam distillation from the grass	general tonic, stimulates circulation in cellulite conditions, digestive problems, tired aching muscles, respiratory conditions, fatigue	sedative, antiseptic, antifungicidal, insect repelling properties, antidepressant, bactericidal, tonic, headaches, stress, acne, skin infections	can cause skin irritation and sensitisation therefore use in low dilutions
marjoram (middle note)	steam distillation of the dried flowering herb	chilblains, bruises, arthritis, muscular aches and pains, sprains and strains, respiratory ailments, constipation, absence of periods outside pregnancy, painful menstruation, colds and flu, headaches, high blood pressure, insomnia, migraine,	analgesic, antioxidant, antiseptic, bactericidal, carminative, digestive, emmenagoguic, expectorant, fungicidal, hypotensive, laxative, nervine, sedative and vasodilator	avoid during pregnancy

Table 9.4 (continued)

Essential oil	Extraction	Uses	Properties	Caution
marjoram (continued)		nervous tension and other stress related disorders		
melissa (middle note)	steam distillation from leaves and tops	insomnia, tension, stress, asthma, menstrual pain	soothing, calming, good general tonic, uplifting and refreshing	only buy Melissa officinalis – cheaper version
neroli (base note)	steam distillation from the blooms	stress, shock, muscular tension, nervousness, dry/sensitive skins, scars, stretch marks, acne, insomnia	soothing, antiseptic, bactericidal, strengthens the nervous system, antidepressant, tonic	an expensive oil so beware of blended versions
orange	expression of the outer rind	colds, flu, digestive conditions, nervous tension and depression, insomnia, dry skin types	antispasmodic, antiseptic, tonic, bactercidal, stimulant, antidepressant, mild sedative	phototoxic
patchouli	steam distillation from the dried flowers	fluid retention, poor circulation, muscular aches and pains, stress related conditions. Particularly good for both bacterial and fungal skin infections	anti-inflammatory, diuretic, sedative antiseptic, fungicidal, astringent, this oil improves with age	highly odiferous therefore use sparingly
peppermint (top note)	steam distillation of the flowering tops	bruises, sprains and strains, swellings, ringworm, scabies, toothache, respiratory disorders, colic, indigestion, irritable bowel syndrome, nausea, colds and flu, fainting, headaches, mental fatigue and migraine	analgesic, anti-inflammatory, antispasmodic, astringent, antiseptic, carminative, emmenagoguic, antiviral, expectorant, digestive, diuretic, hepatic,nervine, stimulant and sudorific	as the oil promotes menstruation avoid during the first few months of pregnancy. May irritate sensitive skin
petitgrain (top note)	steam distillation of the leaves and twigs	oily skin and hair, indigestion, flatulence, insomnia, premenstrual syndrome, nervous exhaustion and other stress related disorders	antiseptic, antispasmodic, deodorant, digestive, nervine and tonic	none

Essential oil	Extraction	Uses	Properties	Caution
rose (base note)	steam distillation or solvent extraction from the petal	thread veins, conjunctivitis, eczema, palpitations, respiratory ailments, liver congestion, nausea, irregular menstruation, excessive menstruation, depression, insomnia, headaches, premenstrual syndrome, nervous tension and other stress related disorders	antiseptic, anti-inflammatory, antiviral, astringent, bactericidal, emmenagoguic, hepatic, laxative, sedative and tonic	rose absolute is more likely to cause skin irritation on hypersensitive skin
rosemary (middle note)	steam distillation of the flowering tops	oily skin, dandruff, to promote growth of healthy hair, head lice, insect repellent, scabies, respiratory ailments, muscular aches and pains, rheumatism, poor circulation, painful menstruation, colds and flu, headaches, mental fatigue, depression, nervous exhaustion and other stress related disorders	analgesic, antioxidants, anti-rheumatic, carminative, diuretic, emmenagoguic, fungicidal, hypertensive, parasiticidal, stimulant of the adrenal cortex and vulnerary	avoid during pregnancy and do not use on anyone with high blood pressure. Rosemary can also trigger epileptic attacks and can irritate sensitive skin
sandalwood (base note)	steam distillation from the roots and heartwood	acne, eczema, cracked and chapped lips, respiratory ailments, laryngitis, cystitis, nausea, insomnia, premenstrual syndrome, depression and other stress related disorders	antidepressant, anti-inflammatory, antiseptic, antispasmodic, astringent, bactericidal, carminative, diuretic, expectorant, fungicidal, insecticidal, tonic and sedative	can cause dermatitis if applied neatly on the skin
tea tree (top note)	steam distillation of the leaves and twigs	acne, athlete's foot, abscesses, cold sores, dandruff, ringworm, warts, burns, wounds, insect bites and stings, respiratory ailments, colds and flu, thrush and cystitis. Can use directly on the skin	antiseptic, anti-inflammatory, antibiotic, antiviral, fungicidal and parasiticidal	some minor skin reactions have been reported on certain skin types

Table 9.4 (continued)

Essential oil	Extraction	Uses	Properties	Caution
thyme	steam distillation from tops of flowers and leaves	respiratory problems – asthma, catarrh, colds, flu, sore throats; cystitis; digestive problems – diarrhoea, flatulence; stress; cellulite	antiseptic, astringent, diuretic, tonic, antitoxic, carmative, immunostimulant	avoid during pregnancy or in cases of high blood pressure, may cause skin irritation and sensitisation
ylang-ylang (base note)	distillation of the fresh flowers	insomnia, anxiety, panic attacks, hormonal problems	sedative, calming, aphrodisiac, antiseptic, tonic helps to build up immune system, hormone regulator, antidepressant	can give headaches to client and/or therapist because of its sickly sweet smell. Can cause sensitisation

Carrier or fixed oils

Fixed oils are very different from essential oils. They are less volatile, hence their use as carrier oils.

Table 9.5 *Carrier oils*

Properties	Carrier oils	Essential oils
smell	very little smell	pleasant
volatility	low	high
soluble in alcohol	no	yes
viscosity	medium	low

Essential oils must be mixed with an oily medium before they are massaged into the skin. The skin will absorb fat-soluble substances more readily than water-based substances, therefore essential oils will be absorbed more efficiently if applied to the skin after being blended with a carrier oil. The most effective carrier oils for massage are vegetable based. Mineral oils such as baby oil are not suitable as the molecular structures are too large for them to penetrate through the epidermis.

Any vegetable oil can be used as a carrier oil but one that has been cold pressed and not processed is the most suitable, as it contains all the valuable nutrients for the body and will not adversely affect the properties of the essential oil it is blended with. Creams can also be used to blend essential oils prior to a massage, and although a vegetable oil is more effective for this purpose, creams can be ideal on smaller areas such as the face, feet and hands.When a cream is used, it should ideally be non-perfumed and unmedicated. Less essential oils are needed when blending with base creams due to their denser consistency: use about one drop of essential oil per five grams of cream and blend with a glass rod.

Extraction of carrier oils

Solvent extraction

Solvents such as petroleum are heated and washed through plant material dissolving any oil that is present. The solvents are evaporated, leaving the refined oil that will be suitable for aromatherapy massage.

Table 9.6 *Carrier oils for use in aromatherapy massage*

Carrier oil / Extraction / Colour	Properties / uses	Caution
wheat germ cold pressed orange	heavy, rich in vitamins E and C. Particularly good for dry and mature skin types. Add to other blends, as it will prolong their shelf life	avoid if client is allergic to wheat
almond oil warm pressed	light textured. Particularly good for facial massage on dry, sensitive skins. [Almond trees that bear white blossoms produce bitter almonds and the pink blossoms produce sweet almond]	
evening primrose pale yellow	ideal for irritated skin conditions like eczema. particularly good for dry skin.	very expensive
avocado green	rich, heavy. Penetrates deep into the epidermis. Ideal for dry skin types. High in vitamin E	thick oil, usually blended with other lighter carrier oils. Expensive
apricot kernel pale yellow	very nourishing, ideal for facial massage	
grapeseed pale yellow/green	inexpensive. Light can be used on all skin types	
aloe vera	soothing, anti-inflammatory properties. Good for sensitive skin types.	tends to be a low viscosity and therefore is blended with thicker oils to improve the texture for massage
jojoba cold pressed	semi-solid at room temperature, needs to be warmed in the hands	very expensive, can be blended with cheaper oils
olive oils cold pressed green	soothing	quite thick, therefore needs to be blended with an oil with lighter properties prior to massaging
safflower oil pale yellow	light textured	not a very stable oil, needs addition of an antioxidant, e.g. wheat germ to stop it from spoiling
sunflower pale yellow	contains vitamin A, B, C, D and E	

Cold pressing

This is the method most desirable for extracting a carrier oil for use in aromatherapy. The plant is crushed using great pressure, literally squeezing the oil from the plant, leaving the pure, unrefined oil.

Aromatherapy massage

Consultation

Prior to carrying out any aromatherapy treatment, you should carry out a full consultation in much the same way as you would for a traditional body massage (See Chapter 4). It is beneficial to find out as much as you can about the client's lifestyle, for example whether they are under stress; how demanding their job is and how they cope with this; what their energy levels are like and whether they have any specific problems they would like you to address. You should also find out which, if any, essential oils they have used before.

As with body massage, it is essential that you have their personal and medical details prior to any treatment and that the consultation card is signed by the client. Use the consultation as an opportunity to build a good rapport with your client and to put them at ease.

Do not forget to use open-ended questions and encourage the client to ask questions. You should find out their reasons for seeking treatment, their expectations from the treatment and discuss and agree a treatment plan during the consultation.

At the end of the consultation, you should identify the oils to be used in the treatment. Since essential oils work synergistically, it is most effective to choose one base, one middle and one top note oil. This is not essential, and on occasions you may only wish to use one oil.

Blending oils

After the consultation has taken place and the oils to be used have been identified, you should blend the chosen oils:

- For body massage, you should use one drop of essential oil to each 2ml of carrier oil, i.e. for 10ml of carrier oil, you should use 5 drops of essential oil.
- For facial massage, you should use one drop of essential oil for every 4ml of carrier oil.

Treatment procedure

Having greeted the client, carried out a full consultation and agreed a treatment plan with which you and the client are both happy, you should instruct your client to undress and assist them on to the massage couch, if necessary. You should then blend the oils and wash your hands prior to commencing treatment. Once you have applied the aromatherapy massage techniques in accordance with the client's requirements (see below), you should give the client home care advice, not forgetting to ask the client if they have any questions. You should use this opportunity to evaluate the treatment as discussed in Chapter 4. You should then assist the client from the massage couch and leave them to shower and dress. While they are doing this, you should add any comments to the client's record card, including oils used and home care advice given, and make their next appointment if appropriate.

The client may be advised to use essential oils in the bath as part of their home care. It is important to dissolve the essential oil in a carrier oil or alcohol prior to adding it to bath water to prevent skin irritation. They should add 6–8 drops to a full bath.

Techniques

The massage techniques used in aromatherapy massage are designed to get the oils into the body, warm the body so the oils are more easily absorbed into the skin and relax the client.

There are three types of massage that can be used:

Shiatsu

Shiatsu massage employs a range of Oriental massage techniques. The strokes relate to the energy pathways within the body. An adapted form of Shiatsu is often incorporated into the aromatherapy massage. The techniques used are long flowing strokes applied to the meridian lines or tsubo (pressure points). These are applied very firmly.

Neuromuscular

This massage technique is designed to stimulate the nerves. The strokes are firmer and applied in the direction of the sensory nerve roots rather than in the direction of the blood and lymph flow.

Swedish

This type of massage includes the following techniques:

- effleurage
- petrissage
- tapotement
- vibrations

These are used to increase the blood and lymph circulation and can either relax or stimulate the client. This massage is the focus of the rest of this chapter.

Order of work

It is always better to start on the back, as this is the largest area and the oils will begin to penetrate through the skin into the blood stream very quickly

You should then progress in the following order:

- back
- back of legs
- neck and chest
- face (optional)
- arms
- abdomen
- front of legs

It is advisable to carry out a friction rub on each area before beginning massage. This is done by using the flat palms of the hands and rubbing backwards and forwards. A friction rub helps to warm the skin and brush off dry, superficial skin cells, therefore aiding efficient absorption of the oils.

Procedure

Back

1 Apply oil.
2 In the stride standing position, perform friction rub.
3 Effleurage reverse effleurage – Standing at the client's

head, effleurage from the back of the neck down either side of the spine, across the base of the back and back up to the starting position. (6 times)

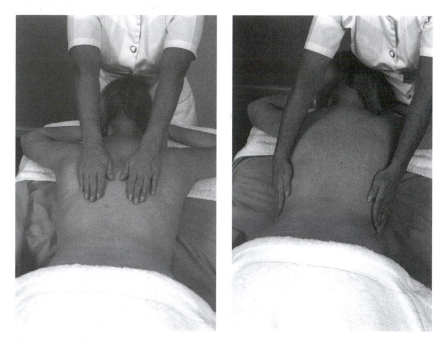

Reverse effleurage, step 3

4   Effleurage downwards – Standing at the side of the client in the walk standing position, start from the base of the back and effleurage up either side of the spine, across the shoulders and back down to the starting position. (6 times)

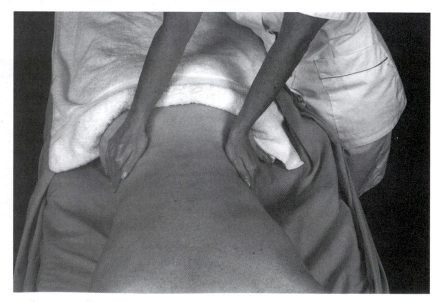

Effleurage downwards, step 4

5 Deep reinforced kneading – Standing behind the client in the stride standing position, place one hand on top of the other and massage first around one scapula and then the other in one flowing movement forming a figure of eight. (10 times, very slowly)

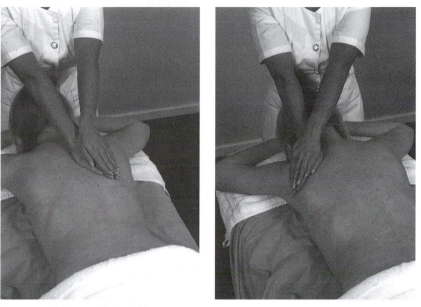

Deep reinforced kneading, step 5

6 Flat-handed kneading – Starting at one shoulder, in walk standing, place hands side by side and knead together, compressing the tissue between the hands. Work hands down to base of the back and slide back up to the starting position. Move slightly towards the trapezius area and work down again to the base of the back. Continue until all the back has been covered. It usually it takes about 3/4 rows to do this. (3 times)

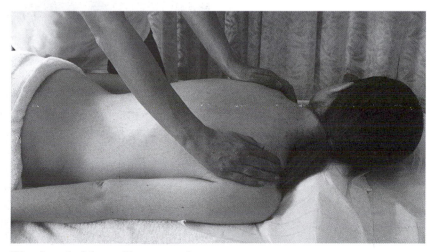

Flat-handed kneading, step 6

7   Reinforced kneading to the trapezius (ironing movement) – Walk standing, starting at one shoulder, place one hand on top of the other and knead the tissues. Work down to the base of the back, then slide the hands back up and move slightly towards the trapezius area and work down again to the base of the back. Continue until all the back has been covered. (3 times)

8   Kneading the intercostal nerves – Walk standing, starting at the base of the spine with one hand on either side of the spine, start to work outwards with both hands simultaneously. Using the first and middle fingers of each hand, knead in tiny circles, working gradually to the sides of the body. Slide fingers back to original position then move up slightly and repeat. When fingers reach the ribs the kneading should continue in between the ribs on the intercostal nerves and fingers slide back on the rib. Continue until you reach the occiput. (2 times)

9   Single-handed stroking to intercostal nerves – Stride standing, start at the bottom of spine using the whole hand alternately stroke away from the spine in the direction of intercostal nerves. Stroke down one side of spine and then repeat on the other side. (2 times)

10   Thumb kneading to errector spinae – Walk standing, starting at base of spine place thumbs one in front of

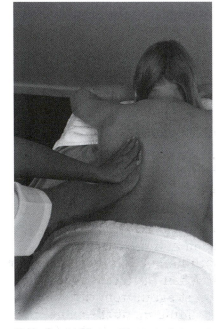

Reinforced kneading to the trapezius, step 7

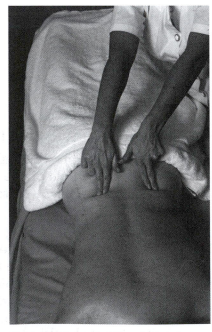

Kneading to the intercostals nerves, step 8

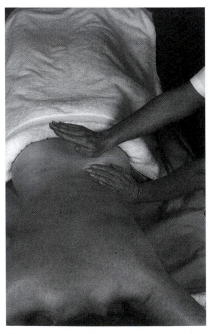

Single-handed stroking to the intercostal nerves, step 9

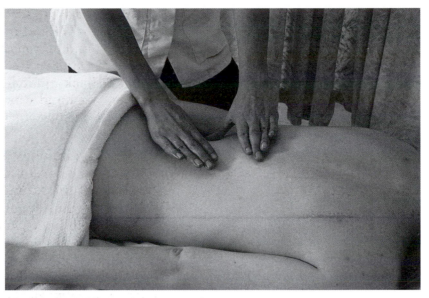

Thumb kneading to errector spinae, step 10

the other on the errector spine. Slowly circle thumbs, moving up the muscle. Repeat on the other side. (3 times)

11 Double-handed stroking to intercostal nerves – Walk standing, place both hands on either side of spine gently stroke both hands out simultaneously in the direction of the intercostal nerves. Repeat movement whilst working down towards the base of spine. (3 times)

12 Repeat Steps 3 and 4.

Back of legs

1 Apply oil

2 Stride standing, perform friction rub

3 a Effleurage – In the walk standing position and using the whole of the hands, effleurage the whole leg starting from the toes working up to the gluteals. (3 times)

3 b In the stride standing position and starting with one hand on the achilles tendon and the other on popliteal glands, slide both hands up the leg together towards the gluteal fold. When the hands reach the gluteal fold, lift off and start again from the achilles tendon, with both hands sliding up at the same time. One hand should always remain in contact with the client. (6 times)

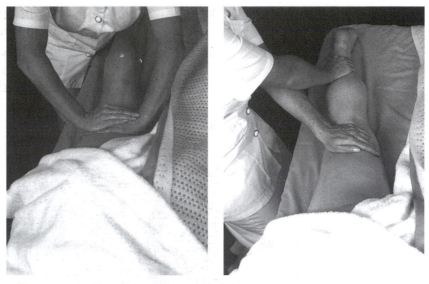

Effleurage to back of legs, step 3a&b

4 Alternate-handed kneading – Walk standing, starting at the top of thigh, hands on either side, knead the tissues in an alternate movement. Work down to and including the foot. Pressure should be applied on the upward movement. (3 times)

5 Covering the whole area, stride standing, pick up and wring the hamstrings. (3 times)

6 Effleurage to lower leg – Stride standing, elevate the leg with one hand supporting the ankle. Stroke firmly with the other hand down towards the popliteal glands. Lift off and repeat. (6 times)

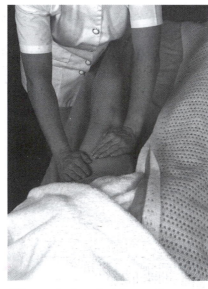

Alternate handed kneading, step 4

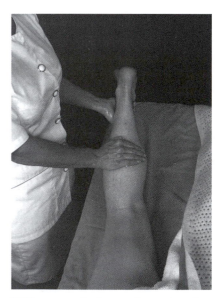

Effleurage to lower leg, step 6

7   Thumb kneading – Walk standing, work upwards to the popliteal glands and back to Achilles tendon. (3 times)

8   Thumb stroking sciatic nerve – Walk standing, place both thumbs one in front of the other on the achilles tendon and slide gently up the centre of the calf towards the popliteal glands. Slide back to starting position. (6 times)

9   Repeat Step 3 a and/or b.

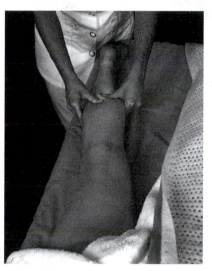 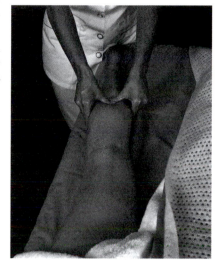

Thumb kneading to lower leg, step 7

Thumb stroking sciatic nerve, step 8

Neck and chest

1   Apply oil

2   Stand at head, effleurage to chest, shoulders, back of neck and scalp

     In the walk standing position, place both hands on the sternum and effleurage out across the chest, behind the shoulders, up the back of the neck and behind the scalp if desired. Slide back gently muscles to starting position over sternocleidomastoid. (2 times)

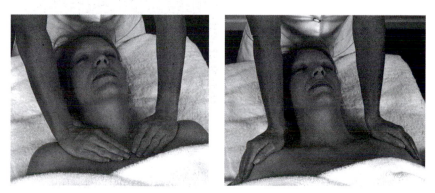

Effleurage to chest, back of neck and shoulders, step 2

3 Knuckling to chest, shoulders and back of neck – Standing behind client, place both hands in relaxed fists with the fingers underneath the hand onto the sternum. Using circular movements, knead out across the chest, behind the shoulders, over the upper trapezius area and back of the neck. Slide gently back to the starting position. (2 times)

4 Alternate stroking – In the stride standing position, apply alternate stroking across the chest from axilla to axilla. Ensure one hand starts as the other hand is lifting off. (6 times)

5 Double-handed kneading – Remaining in the same area, stride standing, perform double-handed kneading, adapting the pressure to suit the client.

6 Repeat Step 2.

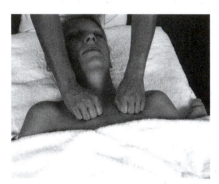

Knuckling to chest, shoulders and back of neck, step 3

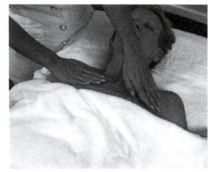

Alternate stroking, step 4

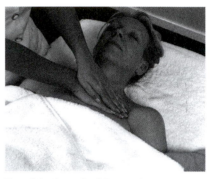

Double-handed kneading, step 5

Tip

If the client is wearing make-up and would like a face massage, the make-up must be removed first.

Holistic face (optional)

If you are going to massage the face and scalp, a different essential oil and carrier oil may be used to suit the client's skin type. Remember to use only one drop of essential oil for every 4ml of carrier oil when blending.

Stand behind the client in the stride standing position throughout the treatment.

1 Effleurage scalp – Place both hands on hairline above the forehead and start to firmly effleurage over the scalp, moving a little further out each time to ensure that all the scalp is covered.

2 Finger kneading to scalp

   Starting at the temple, use the fingertips to slowly but firmly knead the scalp all over. This movement is similar to that made when shampooing the hair, but with a slower action.

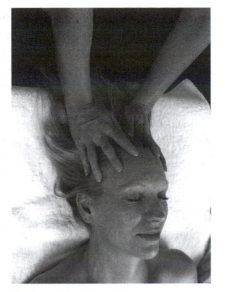

Effleurage to scalp,
step 1

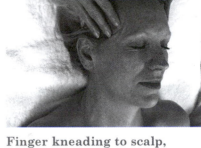

Finger kneading to scalp,
step 2

3   Repeat step 1 a further three times.

4   Effleurage to neck – Place both hands on the sternum
    and effleurage up the neck to the chin, out across the
    jawline, and gently back to starting position.

5   Effleurage across chin

    a   Supporting the side of the head with one hand,
        apply a smooth effleurage stroke with the other
        hand from one angle of the jaw to the other. Swap
        hands and repeat on the other side. (4 times)

    b   Place hands on the jaw move up over cheeks to the
        temples. Circle temples and slide back down to
        starting position. (3 times)

6   One-finger effleurage around lips – With the ring
    fingers of both hands placed beneath the centre of the
    lower lip, apply a light effleurage stroke around the
    mouth to the nose. Take the fingers off the skin and
    repeat the movement three times.

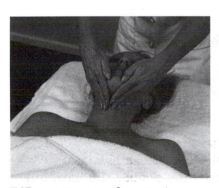

Effleurage to neck, step 4

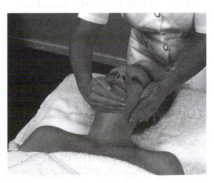

Effleurage across chin, step 5a

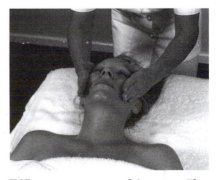

Effleurage across chin, step 5b

7 Effleurage from nose to ears

    a Place the first and middle finger of each hand on either side of the nostrils. With a light, even pressure work across the cheeks and beneath the cheekbones to the ear. (3 times)

    b Place both middle fingers on the bridge of the nose one in front of the other and stroke alternately down the nose. (6 times)

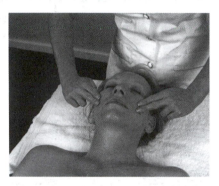

Effleurage from nose to ears, step 7a

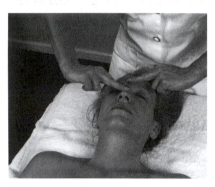

Effleurage down nose, step 7b

8 Circle around eyes – Place both thumbs on the forehead with one hand placed on the side of the head for support. With the fingers of the other hand, circle around the eyes towards the nose. (3 times)

Keeping the thumbs in contact with the skin, support the other side of the head with the fingers of the free hand. (3 times)

Repeat the whole of this step a further two times.

9 Alternate stroking to forehead – Place one hand on the forehead and stroke from the eyebrows to the hairline using slow, controlled effleurage movement. Repeat with alternative hands, covering the whole forehead.

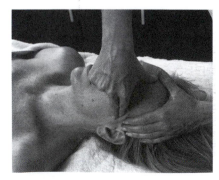

Circle around eyes, step 8

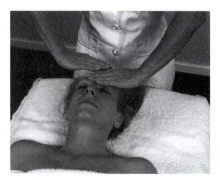

Alternate stroking to forehead, step 9

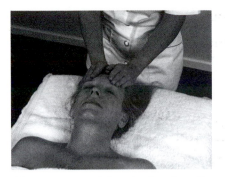

Alternate stroking to forehead, step 10

10 Place both hands, fingers facing each other, on the forehead and at the same time stroke out to the temples. (3 times)

11 Finish by applying gentle pressure to the temples.

Arm

1 Apply oil

2 Perform friction rub in the stride standing position

3 Effleurage to the whole arm – Walk standing, starting from tips of fingers, effleurage to the shoulders and back to starting position using each hand alternately. (6 times)

4 Effleurage elbow to shoulder – Walk standing. (6 times)

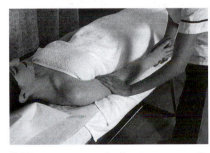

Effleurage to whole arm, step 3

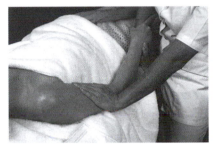

Effleurage elbow to shoulder, step 4

5 Kneading – Walk standing, using both hands, cup the deltoid and knead the area alternately. (10 times)

6 Picking up biceps and triceps – Stride standing, using both hands alternately, pick up the tissues of the biceps and triceps. (3 times)

7 Picking up forearm – Using both hands alternately, pick up tissues of forearm. (3 times)

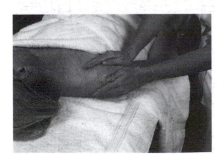

Kneading, step 5

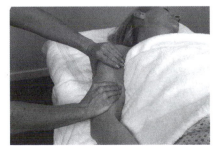

Picking up over forearm, biceps and triceps, step 6

8   Finger kneading – Walk standing, apply circular movements to the elbow with one hand while using the other hand to support the elbow.

9   Thumb kneading to the forearm – Walk standing, covering the whole area. (3 times)

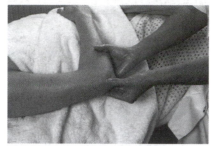

Picking up forearm, step 8

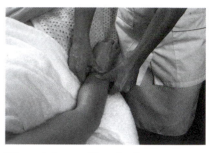

Thumb kneading to forearm, step 9

10   Effleurage to hand – walk standing, alternate from finger tips to wrist. (6 times)

11   Thumb kneading

     a   Apply thumb kneading to the palms. (3 times)

     b   Apply thumb kneading to the back of the hand. (3 times)

     c   Apply thumb kneading to the wrist bone. (6 times)

     d   Apply thumb kneading to the tendons on top of the hand. (3 times)

12   Repeat Step 3.

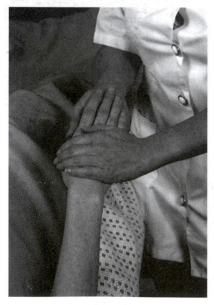

Effleurage to hand, step 10

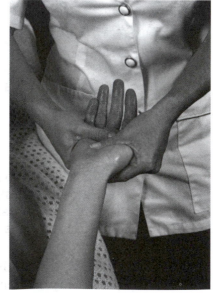

Thumb kneading to palm, step 11a

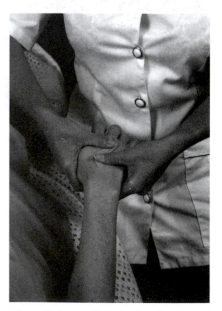

Thumb kneading to back of hand, step 11b

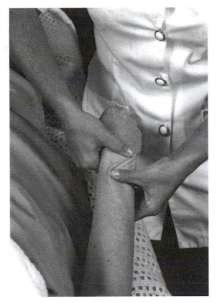

Thumb kneading to wrist bone,
step 11c

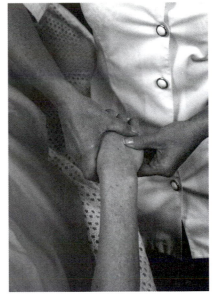

Thumb kneading to tendons on
top of hand, step 11d

Abdomen

1. Apply oil

2 Diamond effleurage – In the walk standing position,
   place both hands on the abdomen just below sternum.
   Stroke out to the waist then inwards towards pubic
   bone. Repeat this stroke in reverse. (3 times)

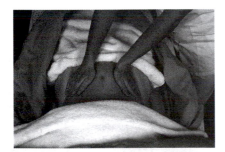
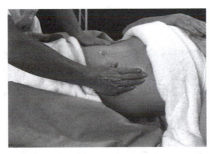
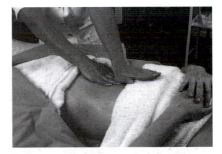

Diamond effleurage to abdomen, step 2

Single-handed stroking to
rectus abdominus, step 3

3 Single-handed stroking to rectus abdominus – In
   the walk standing position, place one hand below
   the sternum and apply a smooth stroke down the
   rectus abdominus. Repeat using alternate hands.
   (6 times)

4 Alternate kneading to abdominal walls – In the walk
   standing position, place hands either side of waist just
   below ribcage. Using circular movements, knead down
   towards the hip. (6 times)

5   Finger circles to abdomen – In the stride standing position and with one hand on top of the other, gently apply finger circles to the navel. (3 times)

6   Finger kneading to colon (optional) – Apply gentle pressure up the ascending colon (walk standing), across the transverse (stride standing) and down the descending colon (walk standing). (2 times **only**)

7   Repeat Step 2.

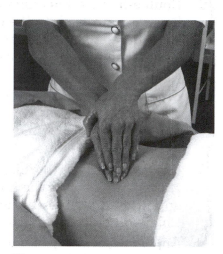

Finger circles to abdomen, step 5

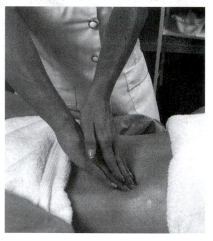

Finger kneading to colon, step 6

Front of leg massage

1   Apply oil.

2   In the stride standing position, perform friction rub.

3   Effluerage whole leg – Starting at the toes, walk standing, use whole hands and effleurage up the whole anterior aspect of leg, finishing off at the inguinal glands. (3 times)

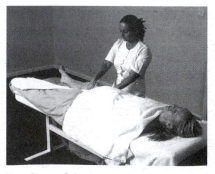

Perform friction rub in walk standing, step 2

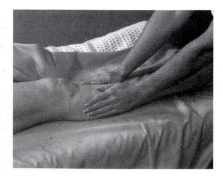

Effleurage to whole leg, step 3

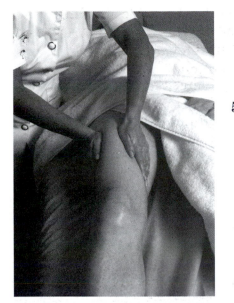

Alternate kneading to whole leg, step 4

4   Alternate kneading to whole leg – Starting at the top of thigh, walk standing, with hands on either side of leg, knead the tissues in an alternate movement, working down to the foot, include the plantar aspect of the foot. (3 times)

5   Reverse diagonal effleurage – With your back to the client, walk standing, stroke from the medial aspect of the knee across the thigh using alternate hands. Perform with light pressure. (6 times)

6   Double-handed kneading to thigh – Walk standing, keeping your back to the client and with your hands on either side of the thigh just above knees, knead the tissues applying firm pressure. Work towards the top of the leg. (3 times)

7   Finger or thumb kneading around knee – Walk standing, using first two fingers or both thumbs, apply small circular movements around the patella. (3 times)

8   Thumb kneading to tibialis anterior – Walk standing, starting just below the knee and using the thumb, apply small circular kneading movements to the tibialis anterior. Work towards the ankle. (3 times)

9   Apply effleurage from toes to the ankle, walk standing. (6 times)

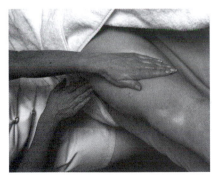

Reverse diagonal stroking across thigh, step 5

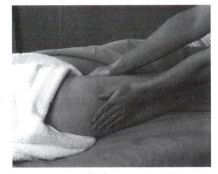

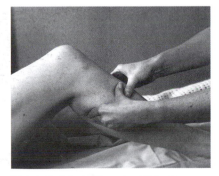

Double-handed kneading to thigh, step 6

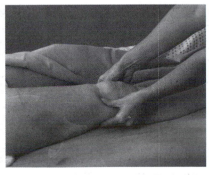

Thumb kneading behind knee, step 7

Thumb kneading to tibialis anterior, step 8

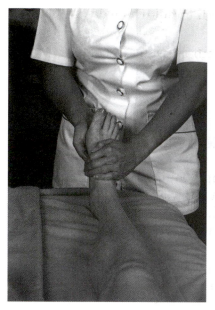

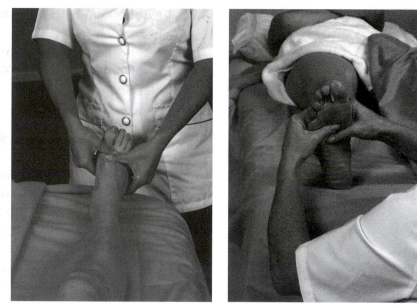

Effleurage from toes to ankles, step 9

Cross thumb kneading, step 10a&b

10   Cross thumb kneading –

   a   Stand at the bottom of the massage couch in the stride standing position. With the fingers of both hands supporting the plantar surface of the foot and the thumbs on the dorsal surface, firmly zigzag thumbs back and forth covering the whole surface, up to the ankles.

   b   With fingers of both hands supporting the dorsal surface and thumbs on the plantar surface, firmly zigzag thumbs back and forth.

11   Palm kneading to sole of foot – Walk standing, support the foot on the dorsal aspect with one hand, use the other hand to apply deep circular kneading to the plantar surface of the foot. Movements should be deep and slow. (3 times)

12   Kneading around the ankle bones – Walk standing, using the first two fingers of both hands, circle around

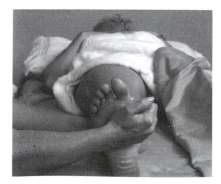

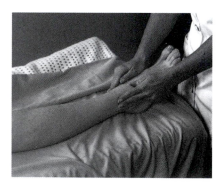

Palm kneading to sole of foot, step 11

Kneading around the ankle bones, step 12

the ankle bones using small circular movements. (10 times)

13 Walk standing, apply thumb frictions in between tendons on top of the foot.

14 Repeat Step 3 six times.

Contraindications to aromatherapy

- Some essential oils bring about extreme relaxation and can make the client drowsy. Clients who react in this way should be advised not to drive home or operate any machinery until they feel sufficiently alert to do so.

- Certain essential oils may cause some clients to experience headaches or feelings of light-headedness.

It is essential that you ask the client to report any adverse effects immediately so that notes not to use these oils in any future treatment can be added to the client's record card.

Knowledge review – aromatherapy massage

1 How do essential oils enter the body?

2 Describe the differences between top, middle and base note essential oils.

3 Explain the properties of an essential oil.

4 What are the risks of using an undiluted oil on the skin?

5 Name six contraindications to aromatherapy.

6 State four contraindications to essential oils.

7 What aftercare advice should be given to a client after an aromatherapy treatment?

8 Describe three physiological effects of essential oils on the body.

9 Name four oils that could achieve the following effects: relaxation, stimulation, upliftment.

10 What carrier oil would be most suitable for a client with eczema?

Body massage case studies

This chapter offers a selection of case studies representative of those which you might come across while practising body massage. They demonstrate the effectiveness of massage and give an insight into the kind of feedback you can expect from clients. Each of the following case studies covers a period of four treatments.

Case studies

Case study 1

GENDER: Female

AGE: 47 years

OCCUPATION: Nurse

REASONS FOR TREATMENT: High blood pressure and pain in left shoulder

FREQUENCY OF VISITS: Once a week, due to time constraints arising from working a shift pattern

GENERAL INFORMATION:

- Marion works as a nurse in a community home for psychiatric patients. Her job is very demanding, both mentally and physically and she has to work shifts which include night duty. On some occasions, her feet swell due to long periods of standing.
- Marion is quite fit and tends to do a lot of walking when she has the time.
- During the consultation, I discovered Marion had high blood pressure and therefore requested permission from her doctor for massage treatment. When she returned the following week, she had a letter from her doctor giving his consent for massage, as he thought this would be beneficial to her.

First treatment:

- A full body massage was carried out, omitting tapotement movements, as Marion had stated she wanted a relaxing and not a stimulating massage.
- Her left shoulder was very tender. This turned out to be tension nodules, which I only worked on for a short time (to try and disperse the tension), as Marion found the area very tender. Conversation revealed that this condition was probably at least partially due to lifting at work so at the end of the session, we discussed lifting techniques.
- Despite being extremely apprehensive at the start, Marion said that she thoroughly enjoyed the massage

Outcome of first treatment: At the second session, Marion reported that after the first session, she became very conscious every time she lifted anything heavy at work and made a special effort to do it correctly, which seemed to have helped the shoulder. She reported that after the massage her shoulder was extremely sore for a few days, but after this had passed, she noticed an improvement.

Second treatment: I carried out the full massage, concentrating on the left shoulder for a little longer than the previous treatment, as this seemed to have increased her mobility slightly.

Outcome of second treatment: Marion reported that the shoulder was not as painful at the beginning of the week, but as the week went on it started to niggle slightly.

Third treatment: Marion's shoulder seemed to be a lot better. The mobility had increased, and it was not as painful. I still spent more time massaging the shoulder area, which was beginning to feel a lot more supple.

Outcome of third treatment: Marion felt her shoulder had greatly improved.

Fourth treatment: Another full massage treatment was carried out, still omitting any stimulating movements. There was no need to spend any extra time on the shoulder as it had improved considerably. During this massage I spent more time on Marion's legs, as her feet were very swollen from being on them for long periods of time since work had been very hectic. Lymph drainage was applied to reduce the oedema.

CONCLUSION:

- Marion felt she was no longer feeling stressed at work particularly in the first few days following a massage. If she felt herself getting worked up, she would practise breathing exercises.
- Marion continued to be aware of correct lifting techniques at work, and this prevented any further problems with her shoulder.
- Marion continues to have a weekly massage.

Case study 2

GENDER: Female

AGE: 62 years

OCCUPATION: Retired teacher

REASONS FOR TREATMENT: Car accident a few years ago and arthritis

FREQUENCY OF VISITS: Once a week

GENERAL INFORMATION Shirley was involved in a bad car accident in 1997 when a car ran into the back of hers. She received injuries to her neck and clavicle for which she had physiotherapy. This treatment ended in 1998. Her neck still becomes quite painful and she still has problems turning her head. As a result of the accident and her arthritis, her mobility has been greatly reduced.

First treatment: The first massage was a very gentle one, eliminating all tapotement movements. She particularly enjoyed the hand massage as her joints did not feel as stiff.

Outcome of first treatment: Shirley reported that she slept very well that evening and her arthritis felt a little easier.

Second treatment: I performed a full massage, slightly firmer than for the first treatment but still not applying any tapotement movements. I spent more time on the neck area.

Outcome of second treatment: Shirley felt she had a little more mobility in her neck and said that it did not seem as 'creaky'.

Third treatment: I applied paraffin wax to the hands, feet and the neck area prior to carrying out a full massage, paying particular attention to these areas during the massage.

Outcome of third treatment: Shirley reported that she felt a definite improvement, particularly in her neck and hands which were not as painful. Her neck seemed to have regained most of its mobility.

Fourth treatment: Again, I applied the paraffin wax prior to the massage. I carried out a firm massage concentrating on the hands, feet and neck areas.

CONCLUSION:

- Shirley reports feeling far more relaxed and her pain has eased.
- She now uses paraffin wax on herself in between each massage, as it brings a lot of pain relief to her arthritic joints. She still continues to have the wax applied to her neck and cervical vertebrae prior to the massage.
- Her neck now has more mobility and she can now turn her head from side to side, although it is still a little stiff from time to time.
- Shirley continues to have a full massage every week.

Case study 3

GENDER: Male

AGE: 45 years

OCCUPATION: Lecturer

REASONS FOR TREATMENT: Very stressed and tired

FREQUENCY OF VISITS: Twice a week

GENERAL INFORMATION: Stuart has a very stressful job with a lot of responsibility. At present he is feeling very tense and down. He is also suffering from stomach ache, through stress related constipation.

First treatment: Stuart was extremely apprehensive about the treatment and not really looking forward to having a massage. On this first treatment I massaged:

- His stomach, as he was not in any pain, concentrating on the colon to try and alleviate the constipation.
- His back, and once he was facing down he seemed to relax more. The shoulder and neck region were very tight to the touch with a lot of tension nodules present. I used lots of stroking and kneading movements to stretch and relax these muscles.

All the movements were carried out slowly and firmly avoiding all stimulating manipulations. At the end of the treatment Stuart was very relaxed and reported feeling quite 'high'.

Outcome of first treatment: Stuart said that after the treatment he had gone to bed early that evening and slept really well.

Second treatment: As Stuart did not feel as self-conscious, I performed a full body massage, still concentrating on the stomach, the neck and shoulders. Once the back massage started, he fell asleep. After the treatment had finished, he was very relaxed.

Outcome of second treatment: Stuart reported his constipation had started to alleviate itself, and he was not getting as worked up. As he was now sleeping better, he was better able to cope at work.

Third treatment: I performed a full massage, again concentrating on the stomach and upper back areas.

Outcome of third treatment: Stuart reported that he felt extremely well. He was sleeping very well, having broken the routine of only sleeping for a few hours each night, and was not having any bowel problems.

Fourth treatment: I carried out a full massage treatment. The tension seemed to have dispersed from the upper back region and was now feeling quite soft and pliable. Once again Stuart fell asleep when I was massaging his back.

CONCLUSION: Stuart's treatment now continues on a regular weekly basis. If he feels that he is getting worked up, he has a massage in between regular treatments, but this is occurring less and less frequently. He feels he can cope better with work and has not been constipated for quite a long time and so is not experiencing any abdominal pain.

Case study 4

GENDER: Male

AGE: 25 years

OCCUPATION: Office worker

REASONS FOR TREATMENT: Lack of energy and feeling of debilitation

FREQUENCY OF VISITS: Once a week

GENERAL INFORMATION: After carrying out a full consultation, there was clearly no medical indication as to why Alan was so lacking in energy. He felt he needed a boost: once he got home from work he just lay in front of the television and then went to bed, feeling too tired to do anything else.

First treatment: Alan was looking forward to his massage. I carried out a full massage, using very light and quick movements particularly percussion and tapotement movements. After the massage Alan said he felt very refreshed.

Outcome of first treatment: Even though Alan still continued to sit in front of the television each night, he reported that he did feel better.

Second treatment: I carried out the same massage as the previous week and again Alan said he felt quite invigorated.

Outcome of second treatment: Alan had been out for a walk on two nights the previous week, as he had felt restless.

Third treatment: Once again, I carried out a full body massage using light and quick movements, particularly percussion and tapotement.

Outcome of third treatment: Alan informed me that after his previous massage he had not gone straight home but had gone swimming, which is something he had not done for years. He is also considering joining some colleagues from work to play five-a-side football twice a week. He does not think that he is up to this yet, but is going to build himself up to it.

CONCLUSION: Alan still continues to walk and swim each week and now has a full body massage once a month.

Further reading

Almond, Elaine. *Safety in the Salon* (Macmillan, 1999).

Burnham-Airey, Muriel and O'Keefe, Adele. *Indian Head Massage* (Thomson Learning, 2001).

Cressy, Susan. *The Beauty Therapy Fact File* 3rd edn. (Nelson Thornes, 1998).

Gallant, Ann. *Body Treatments and Dietetics for the Beauty Therapist* (Nelson Thornes, 1985).

McGuinness, Helen. *Anatomy and Physiology Beauty Therapy Basics* (Hodder & Stoughton, 1995).

Nordmann, Lorraine. *Professional Beauty Therapy NVQ 3* (Thomson Learning, 2000).

Nordmann, Lorraine. *Beauty Therapy – The Foundations, (Level 2),* 2nd edn. (Thomson Learning, 1999).

Rowett, H.G.Q. *Basic Anatomy and Physiology* 4th edn. (John Murray, 1999).

Index